Introduction

This new edition of the P. Suurland-photo guide shows you a green country, never in need of water. On the contrary: this is a country that has always fought against the water. The old saying 'God created the world, and the Dutch created Holland', still holds truth. This guide shows you how the Dutch make sure that Holland remains Holland.

These typical Dutch characteristics can be seen everywhere. In the fertile polderlands, nothing is left to chance, as Holland's heir enemy, the water, is always present. In the cities, where well-kept houses display the richness of previous centuries, there are no feudal palaces to be visited. For centuries, Holland's hard-working merchants and craftsmen displayed a strong dislike of authoritarian rulers. Nowhere in the world can the history of trade so easily be traced as in Amsterdam, a city that has kept a cosmopolitan ambiance without becoming a busy metropolis. But let's not forget the charm of other cities. From the Gouda church windows, history looks you straight in the eyes. Edam has a quiet, human ambiance. Rotterdam is the largest harbor in the world.

This guide helps you to discover the charm of this small country. The pictures show you the most scenic spots, and the practical information in the back of this book helps you find them. The numbers on the map of Holland correspond with the page numbers, enabling you to move quickly through this book.

P. Suurland Publishers hope you will enjoy reading this book.

Peter Suurland.

Her Majesty Beatrix
Queen of the Netherlands

Amsterdam

Amsterdam, capital of the Netherlands, is a bustling city with 718.000 inhabitants. Few cities in the world have a historic center as large and untouched as Amsterdam, and you'll find few cities where water is as predominant as it is here. This picture shows the **Magere Brug** ('Skinny Bridge') on the river Amstel, which previously emptied into the IJ, an arm of the North Sea.

The Magere Brug

This bridge was built on the Amstel in 1671. Legend has it that the bridge was financed by two sisters called Magere. Others, however, claim that during the construction of the bridge, construction workers ran out of building materials. When they were about to complete construction, they had only one beam left for the middle part of the bridge. The question as to who is right and who is wrong remains unanswered. In any case, this bridge has become a symbol of Amsterdam.

Central Station

Most visitors will get their first impression of Amsterdam upon arrival at the Central Station, which is situated on an artificial island. The trading vessels used to moor here (see the painting on page 13), until the construction of the station was completed in 1889. A striking detail is the two clocks on the towers marking both sides of the main entrance. The right clock shows the time, the left one shows the direction of the wind. The square at the foot of the station is a lively place, not only for travelers, but also for those who just enjoy watching the travelers come and go.

If you turn round, you will face a much older part of Amsterdam. The water you see is part of the old harbor, **the Damrak**. The tower in the background belongs to the **Oude Kerk** ('Old Church'), the first church to be erected in Amsterdam, in the 13th century. If you're patient, you may hear the sound of the 17th century carillon. The bell-founders, the brothers Hemony, were Protestant immigrants who fled France. They were among the best bell-founders of Europe in their time.

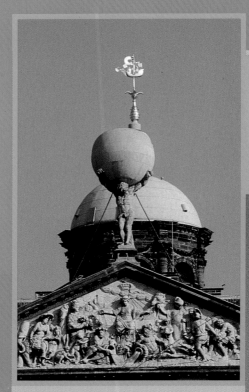

The Royal Palace

The Royal Palace is actually the former city hall. It dominates the west side of Dam square. It was built from 1648 to 1665, during the Dutch golden age, when Amsterdam was the most important harbor in the world. It was to be a symbol of prosperity and wealth. The picture on the left shows the giant Atlas carrying the globe. The architect,

The Royal Palace

The Dam

The Dam is the historic heart of the city. In the 13th century, the dam in the river Amstel was built here. Hence the name: Amsterdam. Or literally: The Amstel's dam. On the east side of the square is the National Monument, erected in memory of those who died during World War II. Nowadays, it is a meeting-point for young people from all over the world.

On the right hand side of the photograph, next to the Royal Palace, is the **Nieuwe Kerk** ('New Church'), built around 1400. The Dutch kings and queens are inaugurated here, but usually the church serves as an exhibition center.

Jacob van Campen, closely observed the proper rules of Classicist tradition founded by Italian architects Andrea Palladio and Vincenzo Scamozzi. Louis Bonaparte (Napoleon's brother) was so struck by the beauty of the city hall that he decided to make it his royal residence. The Dutch Royal Family hardly ever make use of the building. It is open to the public most of the time, and the interior is worth a visit (see picture on the right).

Amsterdam first grew up around the Dam. The first 'Amsterdammers' were fishermen and merchants, who obtained freedom of toll from Count Floris the Fifth in 1275. This is the oldest official record of Amsterdam as a trading city.

The painting from the Amsterdam Historic Museum depicts a scene from 17th-century Amsterdam. On the far left is the city hall while under construction (the current Royal Palace). Behind it is the Nieuwe Kerk (New Church). On the right, in the background, are the houses of the Damrak and the Oude Kerk (Old Church).

Amsterdam's Coat of Arms

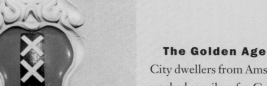

Amsterdam's coat of arms, the heraldic figure bearing the three 'St. Andrew's crosses', stems from this era as well.

Some say the three crosses represent the three enemies of the city of Amsterdam: water, fire, and the plague. The crosses can still be seen everywhere in the city (see pictures on the right).

The Golden Age

City dwellers from Amsterdam often worked as sailors for German Hansa cities (trading cities in northern Germany), until they discovered the possibility of making money working as merchants themselves. In the 16th century, Amsterdam was already a very important harbor in north-western Europe. Wheat from the Baltic area, wool from England, and wine and salt from France were traded here. After the discovery of the new continents, a lively trade in spices began, supplied via Spanish and Portuguese harbors. During the Eighty Years War, these harbors were closed to the Dutch, and they were forced to explore new continents themselves. This event marked the beginning of the Golden Age, and triggered the development of Amsterdam as the biggest harbor in the world, a position that would be held until around 1700.

The Dam in the 17th-century

Canals

More than two thirds of the historic city was constructed during the Golden Age. The characteristic structure of the city originates from this era. In the middle of the picture lies the medieval part of the city, marked by the **Singel**, a former 16th- century defense moat. From 1612 onward, town-planning expanded the city beyond its historic canals. These were among the first systematic planning efforts in Europe.

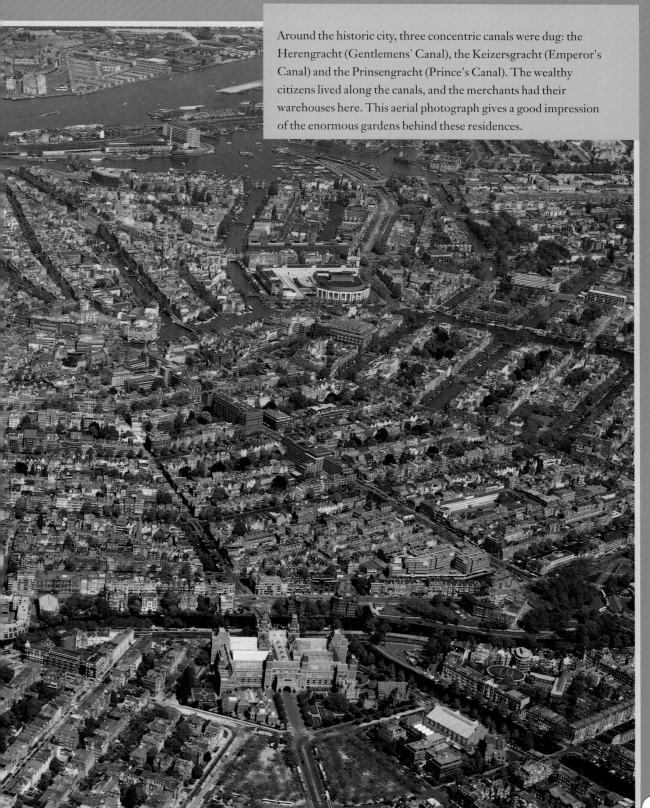

Around the historic city, three concentric canals were dug: the Herengracht (Gentlemens' Canal), the Keizersgracht (Emperor's Canal) and the Prinsengracht (Prince's Canal). The wealthy citizens lived along the canals, and the merchants had their warehouses here. This aerial photograph gives a good impression of the enormous gardens behind these residences.

Trade

The money needed for city-planning and the prosperous canal houses was made with trade. In the 16th century, Flanders was the trading-center of Europe. After the conquest of Antwerp by the Spanish in 1685, trade declined there and Amsterdam became the dominant trading-center of Europe. The location of the Central Station was formerly a palisade, where sailing-vessels moored in order to transfer their cargo onto smaller boats, which transported it to the warehouses. Many former warehouses have nowadays been transformed into luxury apartments, but remain easily recognizable by their shutters. These shutters are actually former loading-doors with glass placed behind them.

Warehouses

The picture on the left shows two warehouses, the 'Sun' and the 'Moon' on the Reguliersgracht, which were built shortly before 1680. Although the front appears to be rather small, these houses have a huge capacity. Both warehouses are approximately 20 meter (66 feet) deep.

The Amsterdam habor, W.v.d. Velde (Amsterdam Historic Museum)

The Maritime Museum

In 1990, a replica of a 17th-century trading-vessel was reconstructed as a permanent exhibition. The original ship, called the **Amsterdam**, was launched here in 1736. It was owned by the Dutch East Indian Company, a trading-company that sailed to Asia and Africa. Dramatically, it sank on its maiden trip to Indonesia, in sight of the English coast near Hastings. The ship is part of the Maritime Museum and can be visited.

The yellow building in the background is the actual Maritime Museum, which was built in 1656 as the naval arsenal of the Admiralty of Amsterdam.

The Amsterdam and the Maritime Museum

Montelbaanstoren
(Mount Alban's Tower)

On the east end of the historic city is the 'Montelbaanstoren', dating from 1512. It served as a watchtower to protect the shipyards and rope-walks from hostile assaults. Nowadays, the tower houses the city's 'water-office', which is responsible for the refreshment of the water that flows through the canals.

For purposes of refreshment, sluices were installed around the city center in the 17th century. Using the low tide in the North Sea at 27 kilometers (17 miles) distance, a current is created by closing the lock doors of some of the sluices every night, in order to prevent the water from becoming odorous.

'Golden Bend', 1680

(Painting by Berckheijde, Rijksmuseum)

Merchants' Houses

The most beautiful canal houses are situated on the 'Golden Bend' along the Herengracht (Gentlemens' Canal), and were largely owned by rich merchants. Nowadays, most of the buildings are offices of banks and insurance companies, the Herengracht truly being the best location in which one could wish to take up residence. The painting above (by Gerrit Berckheijde) shows the 'Golden Bend' just after construction was completed in 1680.

Interior Museum Van Loon

Some wealthy merchant families gathered a fortune in a very short time. They could afford to lead a life of luxury which had its counterpart only in the living standards of the nobility abroad. The residence of one of those families, the Van Loons, has remained untouched since the 18th century. The house was inhabited by the descendants of the family of Van Loon until 1964. These days it is open to the public.

House with the Heads

A showpiece of Dutch Renaissance style is the 'House with the Heads' on the Keizersgracht, built according to a design by Hendrick de Keyser, and completed in 1623. The gable shows six portraits of Greek gods. Tradition, however, transformed them into the heads of three burglars, caught and beheaded by the maid. This house was the residence of Louis de Geer, one of the first European 'steel-tycoons' who, around 1630, founded the steel-industry at Norrköping, Sweden. In his Amsterdam mansion, he accommodated famous philosophers, like the Czech Amos Comenius. At the present day, the municipal service that takes care of buildings of historic interest holds residence here.

Both by day and by night, the canals have an attractive ambiance. Both the gables and the 220 bridges that link the canals are illuminated at night. The picture above shows the merchant houses on Herengracht. The seven bridges on Reguliersgracht form a beautiful pattern of consecutive arches (left).

Reguliersgracht

The Nieuwmarkt

One of the oldest neighborhoods in Amsterdam, just east of Central Station and Dam Square, is the Nieuwmarkt area. This neighborhood is marked by the former eastern city-gate. Built in 1490, its function changed to that of the city's weigh-house in the 17th century. Goods to be sold were first weighed here in order to check whether they weighed as much as the salesman claimed. On the first floor, the members of the guild of surgeons met. Rembrandt's painting 'Lesson in Anatomy', currently on display in the Mauritshuis in The Hague (page 48), originally hung here.

Livingroom of the house with the Hidden Church

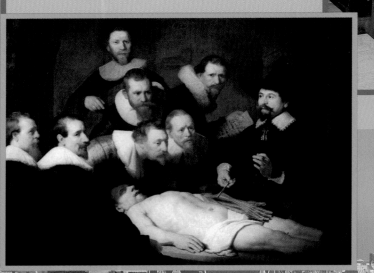

Lesson in anatomy of dr. Tulp,
Rembrandt

Hidden Churches

When the Oude Kerk became a Protestant church in 1578, those who had kept the Catholic faith had to find other accommodations to read mass. For this purpose, rich Catholics often appointed hidden churches in their own houses. These churches were a public secret. Everybody knew about their existence, but as long as they remained hidden and nobody was disturbed by them, they were tolerated. Of the few hidden churches that remain, probably the best example is the one in this house, in the middle of the Red Light district. The 17th-century interior is still intact (picture above), and the church itself is a fine specimen of 18th-century baroque. The name of the church is derived from its odd location: an attic. It is called 'Onze Lieve Heer op Solder', 'Our Lord in the Attic', a hidden place worth a visit!

The Red Light District

A famous attraction of a totally different nature can be found just off the Nieuwmarkt. A visit to the Red Light district is a bit like window shopping. These windows are a necessity in this profession. In the predominantly wet climate of Holland, the ladies might easily catch a cold while they are standing outside, especially in winter.

The Jordaan

The Jordaan is a very special neighborhood. In 1612, the city planners destined this area for the lower middle class and the working class. Companies that were not tolerated elsewhere in the city because of the apparent danger from fire, or the nuisance from noises or stench, were allowed to open business here. Up to this very day the Jordaan has been able to retain its unique character. The dead straight streets with 17th-century houses breath a distinct ambiance. The country's quietness and the city's liveliness meet here, and attract many artists and students. You'll find numerous small shops and boutiques here, as well as cozy cafés and fine restaurants. The Noordermarkt, a market held on Mondays and Saturdays, is also worth a stroll (picture below).

The Westerkerk (Western Church)

The bell tower of the Westerkerk, completed in 1638, dominates the area of the Jordaan (picture top left). This 85 meter (279 feet) tower is surmounted by the Emperor's crown of Maximilian of Austria, who granted permission to carry this crown in the city's coat of arms in 1489. In summertime, the tower affords a splendid view of the concentrically patterned canals. Inside the church is Rembrandt's grave. Tracing the exact spot of it is impossible, as Rembrandt was buried in a pauper's grave. Queen Beatrix married in the Westerkerk in 1966.

Sint-Andries hofje, Jordaan

Hofjes (Courtyards)

Another nice surprise are the 'hofjes', small courts that consist of tiny houses erected along a courtyard. The atmosphere is pleasant and peaceful; time seems to have come to a standstill here. Originally paid for by rich families to house the elderly poor, today they are often inhabited by students.

At the top right is the Karthuizerhof (Carthusian Almshouse), built in 1651. Poor widows lived here gratuitously, supported with bread, cheese and a few nickels every week. Thirty tons of peat were supplied annually for heating. It is currently inhabited by students.

The Sint-Andries Hofje (St. Andrew's Almshouse), founded in 1615, can be entered through a inconspicuous door at Egelantiersgracht 107. A Delft ware-tiled corridor leads to a sublime courtyard and a garden (picture in the middle).

The Anne-Frankhouse

Anne Frank

At Prinsengracht 263, located 150 meters (500 feet) from the Westerkerk, is the house where Anne Frank and her family were in hiding during World War II. Hoping to escape deportation to the concentration camps, they created a construction that made use of the typical shape of the merchant houses in Amsterdam, which was not very broad but extremely deep.

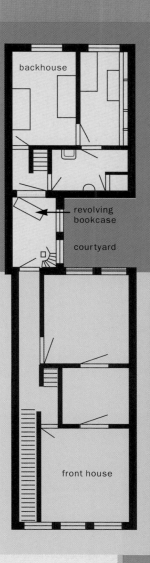

backhouse

revolving bookcase

courtyard

front house

Actually consisting of two houses, the front and the back part are often separated by a small courtyard, and only connected by a small corridor (top right on the map). When the Frank family decided to go into hiding in the back part of the house, they painted the windows at the rear end of the front white and covered up the entrance with a bookcase. When standing in the front house, it was impossible to see that there was another house behind it. The diary which Anne Frank kept describes in detail the family's life underground. Tragically, their hiding place was discovered after two years, and the family was deported. Anne died in March 1945 in the concentration camp of Bergen-Belsen. Only Anne's father survived.

The revolving bookcase.

The Jewish Quarter

Located on the east side of the city center, this is the area where Jewish refugees from all over Europe settled. Before World War II (bottom picture), there were 140,000 Jews living in Amsterdam (of a total of 800,000 residents). The Portuguese Synagogue (top and right pictures) was, after construction in 1675, the largest Jewish building in the world at the time. Nowadays, it is used by the Sephardic community of Amsterdam. The former High German Synagogue is currently a museum of Jewish history.

Interior of the Portuguese Synagogue.

Pre-war picture of the Jewish Quarter.

At the end of the 16th century, Protestants and Jews fled Flanders and escaped to Amsterdam, bringing with them the art of diamond-polishing. Since then, it has become a tradition upheld by Amsterdam's craftsmen. In the 18th century, Amsterdam even held the monopoly of the cutting of Brazilian diamonds. Around 1870, the arrival of the first diamonds from South Africa was a strong impetus for the diamond industry. Despite continuous set-backs caused by recurrent economic crises and growing competition, Amsterdam has been successful in keeping its name as a diamond-city.

Some of the larger diamond-cutteries are united in the Diamond Foundation and are open to the public. The building that houses the diamond company Gassan, (photo above) founded in 1878 as the first steam-driven diamond-cuttery, is now a brilliant industrial monument. The Koh-i-Noor, the famous Indian diamond that decorates the British crown, was polished by diamond cuttery Coster, founded in 1852 (picture right).

The British crown

Houseboats

Totaling approximately 2500, houseboats are a striking presence in Amsterdam's cityscape. Practically all houseboats have gas and electricity, and, with a few exceptions, they are privately owned. Their modern conveniences equal those of regular houses. Purchasing costs rise as high as those of a regular suburban single-family dwelling.

Houseboats are subject to regulations that strongly limit their mobility. Permits are granted only for a fixed location. Municipal policy focuses on stimulating the usage of historic ships as houseboats. Houseboats are particularly popular among artists.

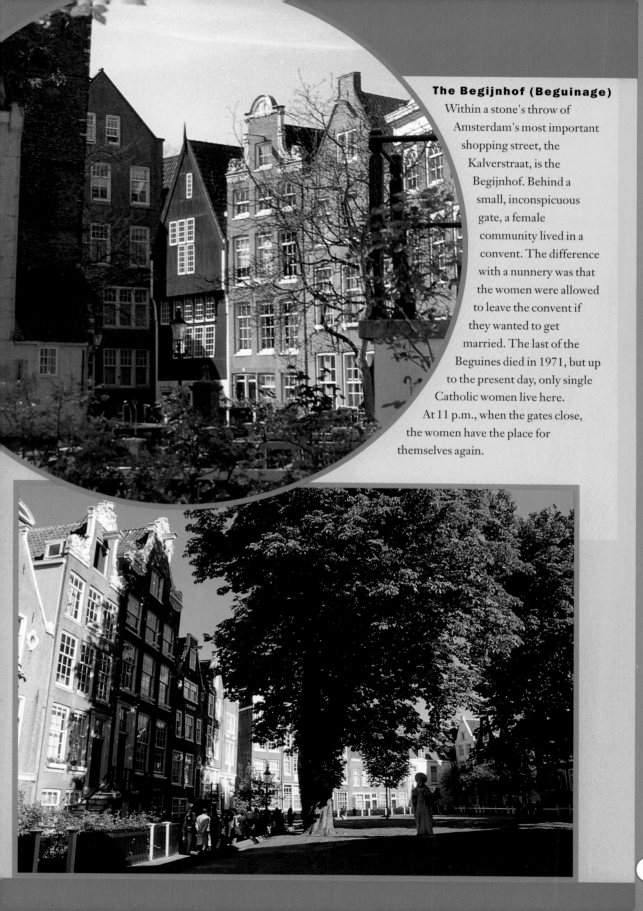

The Begijnhof (Beguinage)

Within a stone's throw of Amsterdam's most important shopping street, the Kalverstraat, is the Begijnhof. Behind a small, inconspicuous gate, a female community lived in a convent. The difference with a nunnery was that the women were allowed to leave the convent if they wanted to get married. The last of the Beguines died in 1971, but up to the present day, only single Catholic women live here. At 11 p.m., when the gates close, the women have the place for themselves again.

Hoisting-beams

One of the things visitors immediately
notice in Amsterdam are the hoisting-
beams on the gables of most houses.
Even today, these beams are used to hoist
big things like furniture, bypassing the
extremely narrow staircases. Furniture
and other goods are hoisted up by use of a
pulley and a rope, and enter the house
through a window. Though usually an
easy method, it gets tricky when movers
attempt to hoist a piano through the
window.

Under close observation, one can see
that most houses are slightly leaning
forward towards the street. This has
three reasons: Firstly, swinging furniture
will be less likely to hit the lower floors
while being hoisted. Secondly, the
houses allow a better view for spectators
standing in front of the house and
looking up, and thirdly, the rainwater is
kept out in this way. Since the house are
leaning towards the street, the rainwater
will flow to the outside of the wall. In this
way, the houses are kept free of moisture.

The City Hall and Opera (Stopera)

Completed in 1988 and situated on the bank of the river Amstel, the Stopera houses both the city hall and the opera. To the extreme left of the picture is the city hall. The cube-shaped upper part of the building is the council chamber, where the city council holds meetings.

The circle-shaped part is the opera house, which has 1614 seats. Ballet and opera performances are held here. The view from the foyer on the river Amstel is splendid.

Waterloo Square Market

Beside the city hall is a flea-market, operating daily from 10 a.m. to 5 p.m., except on Sundays. In 1882, local authorities had a canal filled up in order to be able to hold a market here. Those who have an eye for valuable things can purchase them here at low price (bottom right).

The Pijp &
Albert Cuyp Market

Until 1870, the entire area of Amsterdam lay within the semicircular city moat, the Singelgracht. One of the first districts to be built outside the old city was the Pijp. Building entrepreneurs built houses for the working classes here. Nowadays, many students live in the area. Hence, it is sometimes referred to as the 'Quartier Latin' of Amsterdam. Every day (except Sundays), a market is held here in the Albert Cuyp Street. With a length of 700 meter, nearly half a mile, and over 300 market booths offering a variety of food and clothes, this is the biggest market of Amsterdam.

Flower Market

The picture below shows the floating flower market at Singel, flourishing continuously since 1642. In the background is the Munt ('Mint') tower.

Rembrandt's 'Night Watch'

Without a doubt, Rembrandt's 'Night Watch' (1642) is the showpiece of the Rijksmuseum's collection (page 38-39). It depicts a citizens' militia ready for action. The man dressed in black and positioned in the middle is the captain, who is on the point of giving the order to start the march. It looks as though his hand reaches out of the painting towards the viewer. Next to him, in the yellow costume, stands his lieutenant. The militia's were responsible for the city's safety, and together made up the city's army. The members of a militia had to bear the cost of their own weapons. In practice, therefore, the militia were associations of the higher classes. Rembrandt's group portrait was ordered and paid for by 18 members of the militia and was hung on the wall of the smoking-room, where it darkened over the years. Hence the name 'Night Watch' was invented, almost a century after it was painted.

The Museum Square

The main art museums of Amsterdam are situated very near to each other. The Municipal Museum of modern art, the Van Gogh Museum, and the Rijksmuseum (picture above) are within walking distance of each other. The Rijksmuseum was built in 1885 by architect P.J.H. Cuypers, who was also responsible for the construction of the Central Station (page 6). The section of 17th-century Dutch paintings is undoubtedly the most famous part of the museum's collection, but the section of sculptures, as well as the section of 17th and 18th-century furniture also cannot be ignored. Especially interesting are the dollhouses, which can serve as a good example of how the houses of the rich were furnished in 17th-century Amsterdam.

'The Jewish Bride'

Twenty years later, Rembrandt completed this far more serene painting. In particular, the manner in which Rembrandt made the sleeve of the man gleam is admirable.

Johannes Vermeer was a painter of a totally different kind. While Rembrandt's paintings are full of warm colors and movement, in Vermeer's paintings a total quietness dominates the scene. One of his masterpieces is the Maidservant Pouring Milk (picture right).

One of the greatest landscape painters was **Jacob van Ruisdael.** This is his most famous painting: 'The Mill at Wijk bij Duurstede'.

The Vincent van Gogh Museum

Just behind the Rijksmuseum is the Vincent van Gogh Museum. The collection of this museum mostly originated from the heritage of Vincent's brother Theo. Vincent van Gogh studied Greek and Latin in Amsterdam for a year, in order to prepare for an education in theology which he never even started. Eventually, he devoted himself completely to painting. As a painter, he was far ahead of his time; he managed to sell only one painting during his lifetime. His brother Theo sent him money from time to time, so that Vincent could survive. In 1890 he put an end to his short and turbulent life. He was 37 years old.

Self-portrait, Vincent van Gogh

Bridge of Arles

Wheat field with Crows

One of the most impressive paintings from van Gogh's early period is 'The Potato Eaters', showing a peasant family from the peat district east of Eindhoven. They made a poor living as peat cutters, and their meal consisted mainly of potatoes. Van Gogh brilliantly sketched their gnarled faces and the harshness of the lives of the poor in the country.

The picture above shows the last painting van Gogh finished before committing suicide in France, July 1890: 'Wheat field with Crows'. Notice the exuberant use of colors: In fact, the painting is quite ominous- the sky, the corn and the crows form a sinister kind of movement.

The Potato Eaters

Schiphol

In terms of size, Schiphol, the airport of Amsterdam, holds the fourth place in the rank of airports in Europe. Schiphol carries 28 million passengers and 1.1 million tons of cargo annually. Every year, 160,000 airplanes land and take off at Schiphol. Schiphol employs 43,000 people and its 101.17 meter (311 feet) control tower is the tallest in the world. Investment in infrastructure still continues, since Schiphol wants to retain its place as one of the major airports in Europe.

The story of Schiphol began when the first military airplane landed here on a soggy meadow on September 19th, 1916. Schiphol is actually located 4.5 meter (15 feet) below sea-level, at the bottom of the Haarlemmer lake, which was diked in and drained in 1852.

KLM

Schiphol has been the home base of KLM from the start. Founded on October 7th, 1919, KLM (Royal Dutch Airlines) is the oldest airline company in the world that still carries the same name. Normally, Dutch companies receive the designation 'Royal' only after being in business for a hundred years, but for KLM, an exception was made. KLM holds the fifth place in the world ranking of international transport. It carries 13 million passengers and 600,000 tons of cargo and mail annually. Its fleet, consisting of 111 planes with an average age of 7 years, is among the youngest in the world. KLM employs 26,000 people worldwide.

Amsterdam ArenA

In August 1996, the ultramodern stadium of the Amsterdam-based soccer club Ajax was officially opened. It has a capacity of 51,324 spectators. The roof can be opened and closed, making the stadium suitable for all weather conditions. In the past 25 years, Ajax won the European Cup I four times, and was world champion twice (1972 and 1995). Other teams include the American football team 'The Amsterdam Admirals'. Several major pop acts have performed here. The stadium is located in the southeast of the city, near the Bijlmer metro and railway station.

ArenA

Zaanse Schans

The mills shown on these pictures are currently part of the museum village 'Zaanse Schans'. Most houses in this village were brought here from elsewhere in the area. Some of them are museums or shops, others are permanently lived in. In 1887, Albert Heijn opened his first grocery shop in the village of Oostzaan. His enterprise grew to be the largest chain of supermarkets in The Netherlands, with subsidiary companies all over the world. The area embodies a typical atmosphere of this region in times long gone.

Czar-Peter's house

Perhaps the most famous foreign visitor of the Zaan area was the Russian Czar Peter the Great. He came to Holland in 1697 to learn the profession of a ship's carpenter; the house he lived in is now a museum.

Zaanse Schans

Windmills

In the 17th century, Amsterdam was the largest harbor in the world. The industrial area that was part of the harbor lay along the river Zaan, an arm of Amsterdam's natural harbor.
The main source of energy being the wind, one mill after the other was erected, until the amount of mills totaled

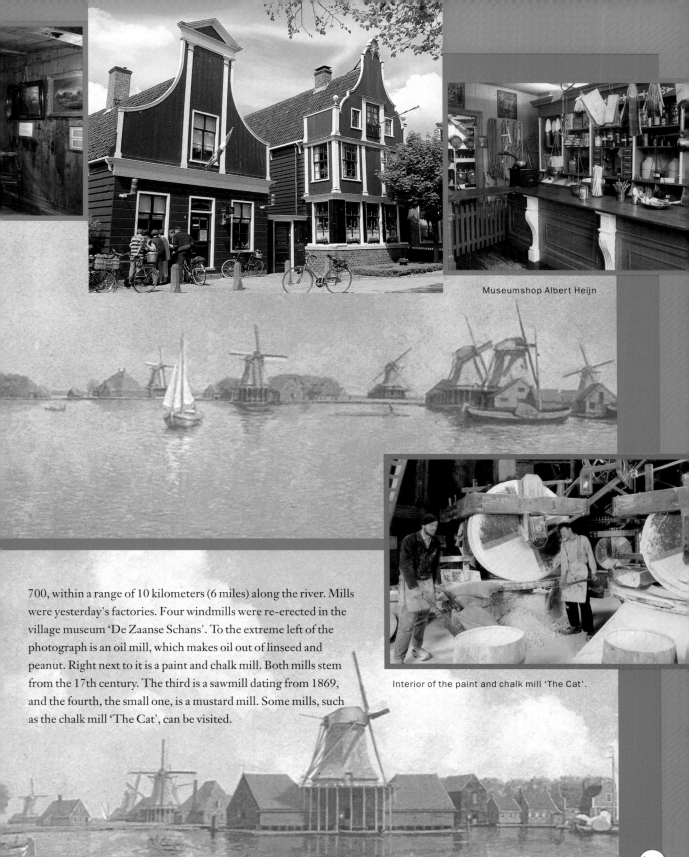

Museumshop Albert Heijn

Interior of the paint and chalk mill 'The Cat'.

700, within a range of 10 kilometers (6 miles) along the river. Mills were yesterday's factories. Four windmills were re-erected in the village museum 'De Zaanse Schans'. To the extreme left of the photograph is an oil mill, which makes oil out of linseed and peanut. Right next to it is a paint and chalk mill. Both mills stem from the 17th century. The third is a sawmill dating from 1869, and the fourth, the small one, is a mustard mill. Some mills, such as the chalk mill 'The Cat', can be visited.

the Knights' Hall

The Hague

Although Amsterdam is officially the capital of the Netherlands and the queen is inaugurated there in the Nieuwe Kerk (page 9), the government is situated in The Hague, and it is here that political decisions are made. Since the 13th century, The Hague is the residence of the counts of Holland. The statue on top of the fountainhead, on the picture above, depicts Count Willem II of Holland. In 1248, he was chosen King of the Holy Roman Empire. The crown on his head and the scepter and the emperial globe in his hands symbolize his royalty. Behind the statue is a part of the old castle, the Knights' Hall built for assemblies and receptions. This is the largest Gothic building in Europe which is not a church. Nowadays, the Knights' Hall is utilized one day a year on the third Tuesday of September, when the Queen reads aloud the government's plans for the next parliamentary year. Over the centuries, the block of houses grew larger. In particular, the view from the pond, originally a small lake, is worth a stop (right picture). The house on the far left, the last in the block facing the water, is the museum Mauritshuis.

Mauritshuis

Currently a museum, the Mauritshuis was built in 1633 as Johan Maurits van Nassau-Siegen's palace. He was the Dutch governor of Brazil around the 1650's. The Mauritshuis is one of the earliest buildings erected in Dutch

Classicist style. It houses the former painting collection of the Dutch Royal Family. Among the most beautiful artifacts of the collection is Vermeer's 'Girl with a pearl earring' (picture right). The stillness, the soft and mysterious light which typifies Vermeer's style, is easily recognizable.

'Girl with a pearl earring', Vermeer

Royal Palace 'Huis ten Bosch'

Queen Beatrix resides at this palace in the Hague Wood, just outside the city. Its construction, completed in 1651, was ordered by Amalia van Solms, who was the wife of William of Orange's grandson, Frederik Hendrik.

Royal Palace Noordeinde

Constructed in 1640 by Jacob van Campen in contemporary French style, Noordeinde is now the Bureau of Queen Beatrix. In front of the palace is the equestrian statue of William of Orange. When the queen is at home, the royal flag is flown from the palace. The queen's offices are in the left wing on the first floor. Left of the palace is the house of the crown prince, Willem Alexander.

The Royal Family

The Peace Palace

The Peace Palace (Vredespaleis)

In world politics, The Hague is not without significance. Since 1913, the International High Court of Justice has its seat in the Peace Palace. Countries in conflict can propound their problem to this court. The money needed for the construction of the palace was provided by the Scottish-American industrialist Andrew Carnegie. Furthermore, many countries provided the International Court with gifts.

Lange Voorhout

The best time to visit The Hague is early spring. In the beginning of March, as the crocuses blossom, the 'Lange Voorhout' (bottom picture) looks like a carpet made of flowers.

Scheveningen

The Kurhaus

Scheveningen is both the beach resort and the fishing-port of The Hague. The most striking building is the Hotel Kurhaus, in the center of the upper picture. At the end of the 19th century, Scheveningen was the most elegant of beach resorts along the North Sea coast, located just north of the fishing-port. The cream of high society from Holland and Germany spent their days here.

'Panorama Mesdag'

This museum gives a good impression of what Scheveningen looked like back in 1881. In those days, the fishing boats lay pulled up on the beach, exposed to the weather (picture below). Nowadays, the ships lie safely in the harbor.

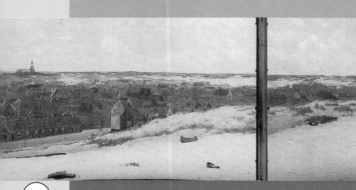

Beach of Scheveningen with the Kurhaus in the background

The biggest celebration in Scheveningen is the annual 'flag-day', the first Tuesday after Whitsuntide, which marks the traditional beginning of the herring fishing-season. The fishing-port is beyond doubt the best place to have a bite (picture left).

Eating a herring

Flag-day in Scheveningen

Madurodam

In Madurodam, a miniature city located in The Hague, you'll find many Dutch monuments made of wood to a scale of 1 to 25, occupied by a total of 10,000 miniature inhabitants. The city was erected in memory of George Maduro, a student from Curaçao who died in World War II.

Both by day and by night, when countless lights illuminate the city, Madurodam is worth a visit.

Royal Palace 'Het Loo'

Apeldoorn

Palace 'Het Loo'

Built as the hunting-lodge of Willem III in 1685, palace 'Het Loo' is currently open to the public. After his marriage with Mary Stuart, stadtholder ('viceroy') Willem III became King of England. This event is known in Great Britain as the 'Glorious Revolution'. Willem himself is better known in Great Britain as 'William of Orange', but he is not the same man as the stadtholder which is referred to as William of Orange in the Netherlands. Queen Wilhelmina, Beatrix' grandmother, resided here until her death in 1962. After that, Beatrix' sister Princess Margriet lived here with her family until 1975. It was then decided that this palace was to become the museum of the Dutch royal family. The picture on the right shows the audience chamber, still in the original state, designed by the French immigrant Daniel Marot in 1692.

55

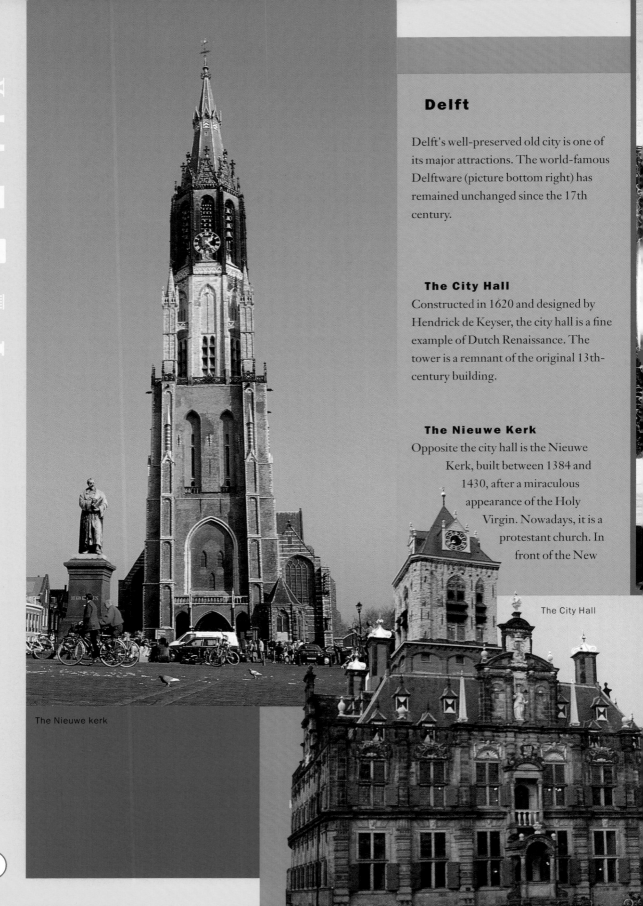

Delft

Delft's well-preserved old city is one of its major attractions. The world-famous Delftware (picture bottom right) has remained unchanged since the 17th century.

The City Hall
Constructed in 1620 and designed by Hendrick de Keyser, the city hall is a fine example of Dutch Renaissance. The tower is a remnant of the original 13th-century building.

The Nieuwe Kerk
Opposite the city hall is the Nieuwe Kerk, built between 1384 and 1430, after a miraculous appearance of the Holy Virgin. Nowadays, it is a protestant church. In front of the New

The City Hall

The Nieuwe kerk

Sepulchral monument of William of Orange

Delftware

Church is the statue of one of the founders of the current maritime law, Hugo de Groot, born here in 1583.

At the beginning of the Eighty Years' War against the Spanish kings (1568-1648), William of Orange decided to move his residence from The Hague to the safer, walled Delft. Ironically, he was murdered here in 1584. William's sepulchral monument, also designed by Hendrick de Keyser, is in the church's choir. William's dog, which once saved his life when his army camp was assaulted at night, rests at his feet. In the crypt of the Nieuwe Kerk is the royal mausoleum.

The Prinsenhof

Opposite the old church is the Prinsenhof (top picture). Originally a monastery dating from around 1400, it was confiscated in 1572, when Delft became Protestant. Prince William of Orange resided here until he was murdered in 1584. Hence the name, 'Prinsenhof', the prince's court. Currently, the building houses the museum of art and history of Delft.

The Oude Kerk (Old Church)

The belltower of this church has been crooked for centuries, 1,21 meter (4 feet) in total! During the construction around 1250, the tower had already started to sink. Attempts to keep building perpendicularly have resulted in the banana-shaped tower (picture right).
The New Church thanks her name to the fact that it is 150 years younger than the Old Church.

The Oude Kerk

One of the few remaining Gothic buildings in Delft is the house of sheriff Joan Huyter, dating from the early 16th century. The decorations on the gable reminds one of Bruges' Gothic. Since 1645 it has been the office responsible for the drainage in the region. The administrators' heraldic figures are depicted over the door.

The east gate, dating from around 1400, is the only gate remaining. The unchanged past is mirrored here in Vermeer's painting 'View of Delft' from 1660, showing only a minimal difference with the present landscape (bottom painting, currently on display in the Mauritshuis, The Hague, page 48).

The Prinsenhof

House of Huyter

The Eastgate

Rotterdam

Visited by 33,000 ships a year, Rotterdam is the world's biggest harbor. It is located on the Nieuwe Maas, an arm of the river Rhine. This river gives the city an excellent connection to it's Central European hinterlands. The annual goods-traffic is 292 million tons. Rotterdam has 593,000 residents, making it Holland's second largest city.

Extensive bombardments during World War II have destroyed the inner city. These days, one of the attractions of the city is the way the old and the new meet here.

Since 1996, the Erasmus Bridge on the river Maas connects the center with the new urban districts, built in the area of the former harbor. A single asymmetrical pier with a height of 139 meter (456 feet) carries the entire bridge. The bridge is sometimes referred to as 'The Swan', after its elegant shape.

The harbour of Rotterdam, right the illuminated panorama tower 'Euromast'.

The City Hall

The city hall (picture right) was one of the few buildings to survive the war. To commemorate the fire of the great bombardment of May 14th, 1940, the soot was left on the gable. Another monument, 'The Destroyed City' by Ossip Zadkine, recalls the misery of war (picture below). The hole in the body of the falling man symbolizes the destroyed city center.

The City Hall

'The Destroyed City', Ossip Zadkine

61

The Oude Haven

The Oude Haven (old harbor), one of
the most pleasant areas in Rotterdam, is
the original river Rotte estuary in the
river Maas. Just like Amsterdam owes its
name to the dam built in the river
Amstel, Rotterdam owes its name to the
dam in the river Rotte. Paradoxically,
everything about the old harbor is new.
On the extreme right of the picture is the
'Spanish embankment', inspired by the
villages along the rocky coasts of Italy.
Due to a lack of rocks, the various shapes
are copied in brick. The ground floors
house several restaurants and terraces.

The 'tree-houses' on the utter right,
designed by the same architect, Piet
Blom, are reminders of times long gone,
when people allegedly still lived in trees.
The four floor-apartments are shaped
like a cube resting on its corner.

Delfshaven

West of the center is Delfshaven, a district where history has remained intact. In 1620, the Pilgrim Fathers left for America from here, reaching Cape Cod on November 4th. That day is celebrated in the United States as 'Thanksgiving Day'.

Delfshaven

Schiedam

Within a stone's throw is Schiedam, home to the world's biggest windmills (picture right). In the 18th and 19th centuries, Schiedam, like Delfshaven, flourished as a center of jenever (Dutch gin) production, and is associated with this national Dutch drink even today. Around the city, 19 mills ground the malt for the gin distillers. Five of them remain. The right picture shows the mill 'North', dating from 1801, and in the background the rebuilt mill 'The Palmtree'.

'tree-houses'   Windmills in Schiedam

63

Puppet pla[...]

City Hall

Gouda

Gouda (71,000 inhabitants) once was a regional trade center with an important cheese market. Hence the name 'Gouda cheese' for Holland's most common cheese. The city hall, built between 1448 and 1450, is a real showpiece. The sculptures on the gable depict the dukes of Burgundy and their families, who were the landowners at that time. At the side of the city hall is a puppet play, showing how Count Floris V granted Gouda municipal right in 1272.

weigh-house for weighing cheese

Right behind the St.-Janskerk is the former orphanage. Built in 1642, it is currently the municipal library (picture right).

The Waag (The 'Weighing-House')

Built in 1670 by Pieter Post, the weighing-house checked the goods to be sold, most notably cheese. On the first floor is a relief by Bartholomeus Eggers that depicts the weighing of cheese. The first floor was occupied by the militia's armory.

Oarphanage

Philips II

St.-Janskerk (St. John's Church)

The main attraction of Gouda is St. John's church, rebuild in 1552 after a fire. The most beautiful stained-glass pictures in the Netherlands can be found here. The brothers Dirck and Wouter Crabeth worked here. The picture left shows a stained-glass picture by Dirck Crabeth, donated to the church in 1557 by Philip II, king of Spain and Holland. At the top of the painting, the consecration of the temple by King Solomon is depicted. The middle shows the Last Supper, with Philip II himself kneeling in the foreground. Behind him is his second wife, Mary Tudor of England, better known as 'Bloody Mary'. The apostle Philippus appoints Philip as the protector of the church.

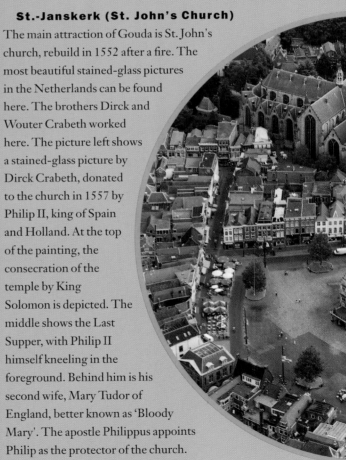

St.-Jan: Window donated by Philip II

William of Orange

The stained-glass pictures of the St. Janskerk date from the beginning of the eighty years war of independence against Spain. When Philip II donated his stained-glass picture, he was still the unquestioned ruler of Holland. After 1572, the situation had changed. His attempts to crush the revolt were not always successful. The stained-glass window on the right shows the relief of the besieged city of Leiden. In the foreground is King Philip's opponent, William of Orange (also on the top picture). Behind him, in the background, are the mills and towers of Delft, the donator of this window. The scene on the bottom right shows someone carrying a barrel of herring to the starving citizens of Leiden. The Dutch army flooded the land to chase away the besiegers. The scene in the middle of the window shows the Dutch soldiers sailing to Leiden (also bottom picture).

Dutch soldiers sailing to Leiden

Utrecht

Inhabited by 234,000 people, Utrecht is the fourth largest city of the Netherlands. In 47 AD, the Romans built a border station here, and in 690 AD, the English monk St. Willibrord established the first Christian church in the Netherlands in Utrecht. Nowadays, the archbishop of the Netherlands is seated here. The 112 meter (367 feet) meter tower of the cathedral, the tallest in the Netherlands, dominates the city. From the solid basement, the tower grows ever more slender towards the top. It seems as though the tower dissolves in the sky. Master Gerhard, the legendary architect who built the cathedral of Cologne, has worked on its construction. Currently, the cathedral is a protestant church.

The city hall (picture top right) consists of five medieval houses. The Neo-classicist gable is an extension of 1830. In 1713, the Treaty of Utrecht, which shifted several borders in Europe, was concluded in this building.

Arches supporting
the cathedral's choir

Drakenborch castle

68

Quays and Basements

The main canel is the Oude Gracht, dug in the first half of the 12th century. Because there was an open connection with the river Rhine, the water level fluctuated. To keep feet dry, the quays were built high above the water level. In 1275 however, the connection with the Rhine was dammed and the water level dropped too low to efficiently load the vessels. For this purpose, a new quay was built at water level. The basements of the houses were extended to the lower quays; their green doors are visible on the picture. It is these two-level streets that Utrecht owes its unique townscape to. Nowadays, most basements are used as restaurants.

Oude Gracht, top: Oudaen castle

Oudaen Castle and Drakenborch Castle

Oudaen castle was built in 1320. Those were the times when neighbor's quarrels often escalated into wars. Those who could afford it gladly paid to fortify their mansions. Legend has it that the residents of Oudaen were engaged in constant battle with the family of the Drakenborch castle, until Frederic of Oudaen fell in love with Cornelia of Drakenborch. Their marriage in 1425 put an end to their family's feud.

69

Oudaen Mansion

In the Middle Ages, the bishop of Utrecht built a chain of strongholds along the river Vecht, an arm of the river Rhine, to defend his bishopric against his major opponent, the Count of Holland. With the rise of Protestantism in the 16th century, life became turbulent. The nobility decided to move to the quieter area around Brussels and sold their castles. The Oudaen Mansion (top left) was the first castle to be sold in 1576, to a wine merchant from Utrecht. The right part dates from around 1300, the left part was added in the 15th century. To this day, the mansion is private property.

House Rupelmonde, Nieuwersluis

Vredenhoff

Rupelmonde

In the 17th and 18th centuries, rich merchants from Amsterdam and Utrecht had country houses built that surpassed each other in beauty, like the 18th-century country house Rupelmonde (top picture).

Vredenhoff

Located just north of Nieuwersluis, Vredenhoff was built in 1751 for Amsterdam steel and weapon merchant Trip. A fortune was spent on the decorations. German smith Hans Lautenschlager was called upon to forge the richly decorated gate.

Vestingwallen

Raadhuis

Naarden

Fortress Ramparts

Today, Naarden is a peaceful city, but in 17th-century Holland it was of crucial importance because of its strategic location. Travelers from the east could not reach Amsterdam without passing through Naarden. North of the city, just visible in the top left corner of the aerial view, was the Zuiderzee. South of the city was an impenetrable swamp. The fortress ramparts, built between 1676 and 1685, have remained intact to this day. In 1923, when the army decided the ramparts were not needed any longer, Naarden was designated as a place of historic interest.

In the Fortress Museum there is still the ambiance of old times. Visit the underground system or the listening-gallery, where you can check for yourself whether someone is sneaking across the city-moat.

St. Vitus Church

The St. Vitus church (in the heart of the city), known for its brilliant acoustics, has beautiful paintings on the wooden ceiling, dating from the Renaissance. Every year on Easter Saturday, Holland's most famous performance of Bach's Matheuspassion is given here. Tickets to the performance are sold out months in advance. On the picture far left is the city hall, a showpiece of Dutch Renaissance architecture dating from 1601.

Jan Amos Comenius

Jan Amos Comenius, the Czech philosopher and pedagogue, is buried in Naarden. In 1628, he left his war-stricken country. After much wandering, he settled in Amsterdam, accommodated by steel tycoon Louis de Geer (see p. 20). After his death in 1670, he was buried in the old chapel of the Franciscan monastery in Naarden, dating from 1440. After the chapel was let out on lease to Czechoslovakia in 1933, it was transformed into the Comenius Mausoleum by Czech artists (below).

Statue of Comenius

Comenius Mausoleum

73

Haarlem

With a population of 148,000, Haarlem is the tenth largest city of the Netherlands. The bottom picture shows the market, with the city hall in the background. The part with the crenelated roof is the remnant of the medieval castle of the counts of Holland. Bottom left are the 'Meat halls', designed by Flemish architect Lieven de Key. The picture left shows a view of Haarlem and the river Spaarne, dominated by the St. Bavo Church, which was built from 1370 to 1490. When he was a boy, the composer Mozart played the organ. Since 1577, St. Bavo is a Protestant church.

Frans Hals

Born of Flemish refugees, Frans Hals became one of the most famous portrait painters of his time. Among his greatest works are the portraits of the militia's, like that which Rembrandt painted (p.38). He was himself a member of the St. George Militia, and painted their portrait after their return from a military expedition to Heusden (p.122) in 1627. Hals' mastery lies in his ability to paint in a very lively manner. It seems as though the characters on his paintings are actually engaged in a conversation. Many admire his ability to suggest movement

'Meat Halls'

Market square

Banquet from the officers of the St. George Militia.

Frans Hals Museum,
courtyard.

and detail with a single, yet rough stroke of the brush, and because of his special use of colors. He is sometimes referred to as 'the first impressionist'. The Frans Hals Museum is housed in a former old-age pension, built in 1608 from the proceeds of a lottery (bottom right is the facade; left, the courtyard).

Frans Hals museum

Alkmaar

The Cheese Market

As a marketplace, Alkmaar has always been of major importance to the northwest of Holland. The only market remaining nowadays is the cheese market, held on Friday mornings from April to October. Before it is sold, the cheese must be weighed at the weigh-house (top and bottom pictures). Built in the 15th century as a chapel for the Holy Spirit hospital, it was altered in Renaissance-style in 1582. On the ground floor is the tourist office, on the first floor is the cheese museum. To this day, the market is held in accordance with the regulations drafted in 1672. A sales contract is made by means of a ritual that involves

The weigh-house

The Cheese Market

At the bottom picture is the oldest house in Alkmaar, the house with the bullet. Built in the first half of the 16th century, its gable is made of wood. On the second floor, in the upper left corner, is a cannonball. Legend has it, that during the siege by the Spanish troops in 1573, it went straight through the house, missed the lady of the house by an inch, and plunged into the front wall.

The House with the Bullet

haggling. One makes a bid and holds up his hand, the other makes a counter-bid while he hits the hand, and holds up his hand again. This bidding and counter-bidding continues until both agree on the price.

After the deal is made, cheese-carriers bring the lot to the weigh house. The cheese-carriers, recognizable by their white suit, are members of a guild divided in four departments, or 'vemen', which, in their turn, can be recognized by the color of the ribbon on their hats. Members of the guild make a sport out of being the fastest cheese-carrier. Quite a difficult task if you keep in mind that a loaded pallet of cheese weighs around 160 kilo (320 pounds).

Hoofdtoren

OT EER VAN HAER GESLAGT TOT LOF VAN
DIE KLAMPEN HEM AEN BOORT DIE WETEN
IER IS EEN HOORNS HOP, DAER GAET 'T OP

Hoorn

Hoorn retains a vivid memory of the Eighty Years' War of Independence' with the Spanish kings. The decorations on the gables of the Bossuhuizen, actually three houses in the Slapershaven, remind of the first naval battle of that war (top picture), won by the Dutch. The name of the houses is derived from the Spanish Admiral Bossu, who was made a prisoner of war in this battle. Top left is the Hoofdtoren (Main Tower), built in 1532 to protect the city from assaults from the sea side. The bell tower was added in 1651.

'Skutsjes' on the IJsselmeer

BOSSU - ZEESLAG
D IO M D II DAG 1573

AAD
WEL RAEDT
EGHTEN

DAER SIET MEN 'T EENE SCHIP VAST AEN 'T ANDER HEGHTEN
DAER SIET MEN REGHTE LIEFDE DAER DOET MEN ONDERSTANT
DAER VEGHT MEN SONDER GELT VOOR 'T LIEVE VADERLAND

Nowadays, the harbor of Hoorn is a meeting point for sailing boats. Former cargo and fishing vessels dating from the beginning of this century in particular are hired out as pleasure-crafts (picture bottom left).

In the 16th and 17th centuries, Hoorn developed into an important city. The meeting-room of the seven cities north of Amsterdam dates from 1632 (picture right). The arms of the cities are inscribed in the gable. Vessels from Hoorn sailed all around the world. Cape Hoorn, the southern end of South America, is named after this city. When Indonesia was colonized, a Dutchman from Hoorn, Jan Pieterszoon Coen, took the lead. He established the first Dutch colony on the place which is now called Jakarta. The right picture depicts his statue.

79

West Frisian Museum

'hanging rooms'

Enkhuizen

Enkhuizen, trade city and fishing port, flourished around 1600. When competition with Amsterdam grew heavier and the herring-fishery declined, so did the number of people living in Enkhuizen. Currently, only 16,000 inhabit Enkhuizen, whereas in the 17th century this number was 28,000. The picture below shows the silhouette of the city dominated by the tower of the Zuiderkerk.

Left of this tower is the 'Dromedaris', a round bastion built in 1540. Behind the ships' masts, far right, is the Zuiderzee Museum, which keeps alive the days when the current IJsselmeer, today a fresh water lake, was still part of the North Sea.

On the top picture you see the houses facing the 'Dromedaris', their back-rooms built out. These houses were built on the location of the former rampart, demolished in 1650. To create space, these 'hanging rooms' were built.

The Cheese Market

Edam

In the 16th century, Edam was a prosperous trading-port, located on the current IJsselmeer. Until 1922, one of the most prominent cheese markets in Holland was held here. On Wednesday mornings in July and August the cheese market returns, held according to old traditions. Among Edam's most striking sights are its draw-bridges, like the Kwakelbrug (picture left), and the summerhouses from the 18th and 19th centuries, where the rich ladies drank their tea (picture right).

Kwakelbrug

Edam

Some houses show funny details. The picture above shows the frieze of a house which tells the story of a fisherman who caught a mermaid. Three characters comment on the story: The soldier praises the catch, the monk wishes he had fish like that in the monastery, and the cripple says that such a fish caused him to walk with crutches.

On the right picture is the Speeltoren (Bell Tower), dated 1569. Clearly visible are the bells of the carillon. The church that the tower was part of was demolished in the 19th century. Further demolition in 1972 caused the tower to sink.

Currently a museum, the house with the stepped gable (bottom) is one of the oldest houses in Edam, dating from 1530. The basement actually floats on the ground water. When you enter, it is as though you are stepping onto a boat.

The middle bottom picture shows the 18th-century town hall, currently a museum, as well as a tourist office.

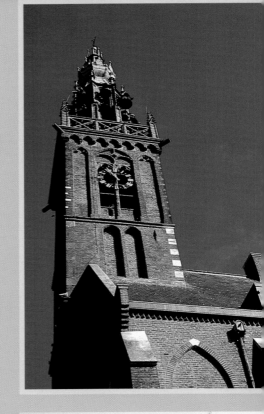

Captain House

The institution which is responsible for the maintenance of the dikes and sluices north of Amsterdam has its seat in Edam. It was founded in 1544 by Emperor Charles V; his arms decorate the entrance gate of the 18th-century office.

On the bottom right are three 17th-century gables. In the 18th century, the lower front of the buildings was replaced, along with the windows. Hence the differing color of the bricks.

e City Hall

Volendam

The old fishing-village Volendam, famous for its traditional costumes, can be a bustling place, especially around the harbor area. The green building in the middle is the fish auction. Since the Zuiderzee was closed off from the North Sea in 1932, the main fishing is of eel.

The main street of this village, the old sea-dike, is now a busy boulevard where people parade. You only need to descend one flight of stairs to enter a totally different world: the Doolhof (labyrinth). Here, you'll find Holland as you remember it from fairy tales, a place where time seems to have come to a standstill.

Doolhof

Around 1900, Volendam was a meeting place of many impressionist painters. Hotel Spaander owns a large collection of paintings from those times (picture right). Many artists donated a painting to the owner of the hotel, Leendert Spaander, in return for a night's stay.

Hotel Spaander, lounge

The woman at the table wears a typical Volendammer woman's dress: a multicolored collar, a striped apron, and a black costume underneath. On weekdays the women wear a black bonnet, and on Sundays they wear an additional white cap.

The picture below shows an image of the harbor of Volendam at the beginning of this century.

Marken

The island of Marken has been connected with the mainland via a dam since 1957. Since the Middle Ages it has lost one third of its surface. East of the island lie the fundaments of a medieval monastery, now at the bottom of the lake, under water on the right picture. The lighthouse, rebuilt in 1839, is sometimes referred to as 'the white horse', due to its shape.

Everywhere on Marken you'll encounter houses that are built on artificial hills, often dating back to the 15th century. This way, the islanders were better protected against the frequent flooding of the land. When the hills were full, new houses were built on poles, so that the water could flow underneath them. However, since the damming of the Zuiderzee, the danger of flooding is over, and many people have built in the space under their houses with bricks to create more room.

The Lighthouse

Traditional dress has been well preserved on Marken (picture left), although it becomes difficult to spot nowadays. The local youth only dresses traditionally on special occasions.

Up to this century, the houses on the hills were built in the traditional style. Packed with houses, these untouched hills are a unique sight. The Dutch government has declared Marken a protected village.

Flower Fields

The flower fields extend over the entire area behind the coast of Holland, from Katwijk to Den Helder. From April to May, the whole region is covered with a 17.500 hectare (43,000 acres) multicolored carpet. Almost half of it consists of tulips. Originating in Turkey and central Asia, the first tulips appeared at the court of the emperor of Austria in 1554. His botanist, Carolus Clusius, fled to Holland for religious reasons. The sandy area behind the Dutch coast turned out to be an excellent breeding ground for tulips, and they soon became extremely popular. People started to speculate with tulip bulbs, and in 1636 the fabulous price of 30,000 guilders was paid for three bulbs. The value of a tulip bulb equaled the value of a canal house in Amsterdam. Shortly afterwards, the market crashed completely. Only towards the end of the 18th century did the trade in tulips start to flourish again. Today, Holland is the world's largest exporter of flower bulbs.

they start blossoming in April-May, they are almost immediately cut to divert the energy to the young bulbs that are connected with the main bulb. In the summer, the bulbs are harvested and dried in special barns, where temperature and humidity is regulated by air-conditioning. In October and November the new bulbs are planted, and the cycle starts all over again. 49% of the bulbs is used in agriculture, either to grow new bulbs or to grow the tulips in greenhouses. The most prominent bulbous plants are: tulips (49%), lilies (17%), gladioluses (9%), hyacinths (6%), daffodils (8%), irises (4%), and crocuses (3%).

Of a total output of 7.5 billion bulbs, 51% is sold to consumers, who plant the bulbs in their gardens. The bulb-growing industry concentrates on the young bulbs that grow out of the main bulb. The cycle is as follows: In late autumn, the bulbs are planted. After the frost, the plants start growing. By the end of March or the beginning of May, they come through the surface. When

Keukenhof

Within a century, the landscape in the bulb area changed drastically. One hundred years ago, wooded dunes and boggy grasslands dominated the scene here. But the dunes were leveled because the sand was needed for city-planning, and around 1900, the bulb-growing industry started booming. One man refused to give up his rural estate. His name was Baron van Lynden, and his rural estate was called Keukenhof. This area once was Countess Jacoba von Wittelsbach's hunting ground, grandchild of the German Emperor Ludwig the Bavarian. The largest part of 425 hectare (1050 acres) is currently a nature reserve; the famous flower exhibition takes up 28 hectare (70 acres).

In 1949, the association of bulb growers for the first time held an exposition in the park that attracted thousands of visitors. Since then, the event is repeated every year. Apart from visiting the flower beds and the greenhouses, the park is a great place for strolling. The best moment to visit Keukenhof is after a rain shower, when the sun comes out again, and the flowers open to spread their perfume.

Aalsmeer

In Aalsmeer, 17 kilometer (10 miles) south of Amsterdam, is the biggest flower auction in the world, supplied with 17 million cut flowers daily. The total surface area of the buildings is 76 hectare (188 acres). After their quality is tested, the flowers are sold by Dutch auctio: the pointer of the auction clock (picture right) starts with the highest price and lowers until a buyer pushes a button to stop the pointer. The data of the flowers, like quality and origin, appear on this 'auction clock'. Roses, tulips, chrysanthemums and carnations are among the best-selling flowers. The auction is owned by a corporation of 4900 florists and employs 1800 people.

Auction Room

The cut flowers are grown in greenhouses, as the climate is to cold for open-air growing. The greenhouses, usually owned by family corporations, have an average surface area of 1 hectare (2.5 acres) and are mostly computerized. Computers regulate the temperature, humidity and ventilation, and since florists found out that flowers grow faster if you talk to them five minutes per day, also this job is often performed by computers.

The strength of Dutch agriculture lies in the shared approach to problems. A good example is the sale at the Aalsmeer auction. Instead of competing, companies exchange information. Thus, industrial piracy is avoided.

Cattle Breeding

As most of the land in Holland is so marchy that only grass can grow there, for most farmers cattle breeding has always been the main source of income. The dominant breed is the Frisian-Holstein, a cow which is especially bred for milk production. A Dutch cow produces on the average 7000 liter (1850 gallons) of milk annually.

Sheep can be seen throughout the year. They are a Texel breed, actually a crossbreed of the English Yorkshire sheep and the original Texel sheep. Wool, however, is a by-product. The main reason for breeding sheep is meat, which is exported to France and Belgium.

A large part of the cows milk production is used for cheese-making. The most famous brands of cheese, Gouda cheese and Edam cheese, are both made of cow milk, although there is a difference in preparation. For Edam cheese, half of the milk needs to be skimmed, resulting in a lower fat content. Edam cheese can be recognized by its round shape. Gouda cheese has a flatter shape, almost like a wheel.

Pyramid-shaped Farms

Pyramid-shaped farms can be found in the area north of Amsterdam. The central part under the high the roof was the hay storage. In the wintertime, the hay got heated, keeping the farm warm. Most farms have a thatched roof, decorated at the front with roofing tiles in a shape that reminds one of the gables that can be found in the cities.

Thatched roofs are cooler in summer and warmer in winter than regular roofing tiles. At the north and east side, thatched roofs last around 80 years. The south and west side, more frequently exposed to the sun and the rain, have to be replaced after 30 years.

Wooden Shoes

Wooden Shoes are the traditional footwear in Holland, shoes being a luxury that only the rich could afford. Still, 3.7 million pairs of clogs are produced in Holland annually. Nowadays, clogs are mostly worn in the country, as they are warmer and dryer than rubber boots. Clogs were formerly part of the traditional dress; you could tell where people came from by the look of their clogs. The village of Hindeloopen had a colorful tradition of painting clogs (picture left), and the wedding-clogs of Marken (top picture), cut by the fiancé, were especially made for that one time occasion.

The Creation of the Netherlands

Dikes and Polders

The Netherlands has always been a wet country. In Roman times, the land behind the low dunes of the coastline consisted mainly of swampland. Around 250 AD, in many areas the sea broke through the dunes. The inhabitants left the west of Holland to return only in the 6th century, when times got calmer. However, around 1200 another period of floods started, lasting two hundred years. Vast pieces of land turned into mud flats, flooded with water twice a day. The first people to stop this process were monks, who built ring-shaped dikes on those sand banks that remained above sea-level even during high tide. Once a dike was built, the sea would deposit new sand and clay against it. In this way, new sand banks were formed, and when they were big enough, they were diked in as well, creating an ever bigger piece of land. The origins of the country are easily recognizable by the shape of the old dikes, which often serve as roads nowadays. The village of Kolhorn, just north of Alkmaar, is a good example (picture bottom left). Until 1844, the sea flowed on what are now the fields at the right of the dike.

This is how the polders came into existence. 'Polder' is a Dutch word, and refers to a piece of land surrounded by dikes, in which the water level can be regulated artificially.
Throughout the years islands grew together, and the mainland expanded, thus creating large pieces of connected land.

The first massive public water works in Holland date from 1287. After Westfriesland, the far northwest of Holland, was flooded, Count Floris V decided to build a surrounding dike with a total length of 126 kilometers (79 miles). Consisting of clay and seaweed, the dike was modernized and raised later on. In its present shape it is still the coastline of the IJsselmeer from Hoorn via Enkhuizen until Medemblik. At Kolhorn, this dike cuts straight through the fields as a 'slaperdijk' (sleeping dike, picture left).

A slaperdijk is a dike that has no permanent function, but 'wakes up' the soon as the main dike breaks, in order to protect the hinterland. The map bottom right shows which parts of Holland would be flooded if there were no dikes.

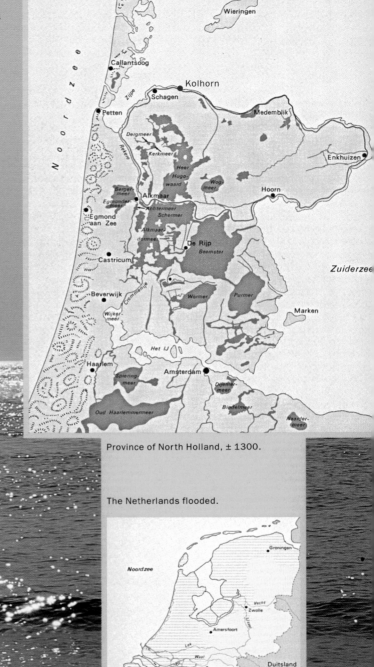

Province of North Holland, ± 1300.

The Netherlands flooded.

The Beemster

In the middle of the 16th century, a windmill was invented that could pump up water. This invention meant a breakthrough in the battle against the water. From then on, it became possible to build a dike around a lake, pump out the water and cultivate the land. The first large lake to be reclaimed was the Beemster in North Holland, in 1612. It took 42 windmills four years to empty this lake of 7020 hectare (17,347 acres).

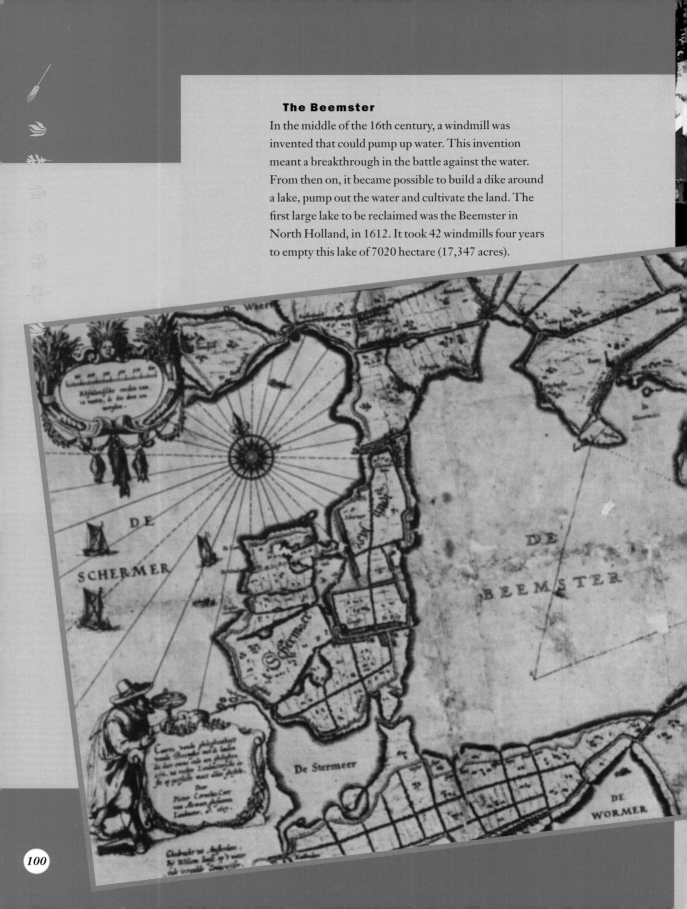

Market Square,
Middenbeemster

The project was paid for by 123 rich merchants from Amsterdam, who thought it a good investment of the money they had made with trade. They built beautiful farms on this newly reclaimed land, to live in during the summer. The farmers themselves could do with the back-premises of the farm. De Eenhoorn ('The Unicorn'), located just south of the village Middenbeemster, is one of those farms (picture right).

Pictured on the maps: Overview of land reclamation since the 14th century

- Sea-dikes and river-dikes
- Land reclamations since 1900
- Land reclamation of the 14th to the 20th century
- Freshwater

Cross-section of Amsterdam and the Netherlands

NAP = Normal Amsterdam Level (Average sea level at high tide)

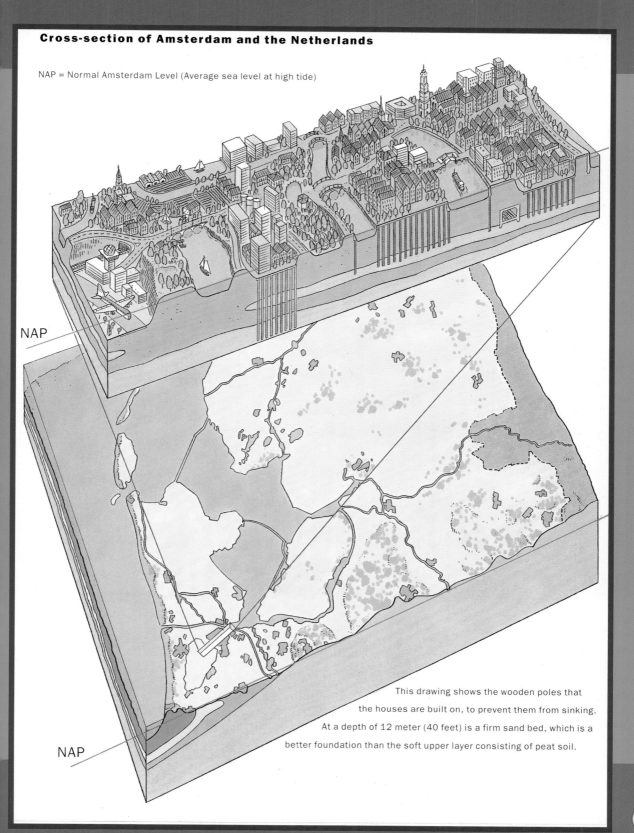

NAP

NAP

This drawing shows the wooden poles that the houses are built on, to prevent them from sinking. At a depth of 12 meter (40 feet) is a firm sand bed, which is a better foundation than the soft upper layer consisting of peat soil.

The IJselmeer dike at Uitdam

The reclaimed land is mostly the bottom of drained lakes. In total, 24% of Holland lies below sea level. The picture above gives a good impression of life below sea level. The houses are based lower than the water level behind the dike. (The picture shows the dike on the IJsselmeer near Uitdam, located northeast of Amsterdam.)

Once a field is diked and drained, both the rainwater and the water that seeps through must be pumped out. If nothing is done to maintain the dry land (rainfall also poses a threat to the reclaimed land), the polders would turn into lakes again within two months. The oldest preventive method is a small sluice that can be opened at low tide, so that the water can flow out. This sluice closes at high tide, prevending the water from flowing in again.

The age-long drainage has caused the land to pack down, and when the water level in the polder gets lower than the water level at low tide, the sluices cease to function. The simplest solution to this problem is to let a windmill do the work. The mill pumps the water into a higher located canal connected with the sea-dike by a sluice, which can be opened at low tide. The sluice remains closed when the sea-level is too high, but in the mean-time, the mill can continue pumping the water into the canal. This drainage method has been practiced for centuries, and continues today, the only difference being the size of the reservoirs. These have expanded over the years, the most prominent now being the IJsselmeer.

The limitations of windmills lie in the fact that they can only pump the water 1.20 meter (4 feet) higher. When the difference in level was larger (as shown on the right picture of the mill at Stompwijk, near The Hague), the mills were placed in a row. Every mill pumps the water into its own pond. As shown on the picture, each successive mill is located a little higher than the previous one, each time pumping the water to a higher step, into a higher basin. The one in the back, the lowest, was reconstructed again after a fire destroyed it in 1908. The others date from 1672.

Windmills at Stompwijk

105

The more serious the situation, the more windmills were needed to safeguard the land. In particular the district southeast of Rotterdam, the Alblasserwaard, closed in and exasperated by the high water level of two rivers, needed relief. Shortly before 1400, two canals were dug to discharge the excess water as far downstream as possible. Nowadays, the in total 19 windmills of Kinderdijk can be found on that place.

By the 18th century, however, the land had packed down so much, that large pieces of land had to be sacrificed. By building dikes, a reservoir for excess water was created, large enough to discharge the water for two months. 16 mills were needed to do the job. Even during a long-lasting period of rising water, it was no longer necessary to let pieces of land be flooded anymore.

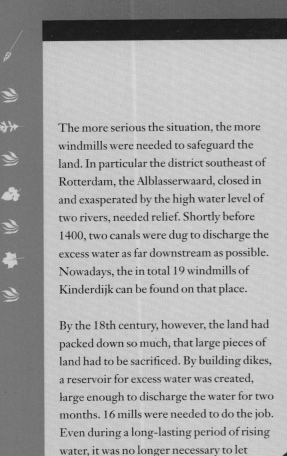

Kinderdijk

The aerial view gives a good impression of the system of Alblasserwaard. The two canals are separated by a small dam. To the left and at the bottom are two series of eight windmills each that pump the water from the canals into the reservoir, recognizable as the swampland on the picture. Under normal conditions, the water can flow into the river. When the water level in the river is higher than usual, the water can be temporarily discharged in the swamps, until it is safe to open the sluices again.

The mills were constructed between 1738 and 1740. One of them is open to the public; the others are inhabited.

Urk

The Zuiderzee Project

The Enclosing Dike

The Zuiderzee was a part of the North Sea that, like a large bay, reached to Amsterdam. Since the 17th century, plans have been made to dam and drain the Zuiderzee. None of these plans ever came into being. However, during a heavy storm on February 13th, 1916, the dikes near Volendam and Marken were breached, and the water reached Amsterdam. Reason enough to start one of the biggest hydraulic projects in the Netherlands so far: The Zuiderzee project. The Zuiderzee was to be dammed and large areas were to be drained. It took five years of continuous labor to built a 32 kilometer (20 mile) dike that connected the provinces of North Holland and Friesland. On May 28th, 1932, at 2 p.m., the last hole was filled. On that spot, a monument was erected, shown on the right picture. The water along the south side of the dam (right on the aerial photograph) has transformed into a freshwater lake: the IJsselmeer, named after the river IJssel, an arm of the Rhine that flows into the lake. The fresh water of this river has refreshend the lake.

The Building of a Dike

Building a dike involves the following steps: First, a dike is built from materials derived from the bottom of the sea. Below sea level, the dike is strengthened with mats, made of wicker and reed. Big rocks keep the mats in place. At water level, the dike is protected from the surge by basalt cobbles, imported from Germany, Belgium and Scotland (picture below).

The upper-part of the dike is covered with clay, on which grass is grown to protect it from the wind and the waves. Consisting only of natural materials, the dike protects the hinterland from flooding.

In the northwest, around the same time as the construction of the IJsselmeer dam took place, the Wieringermeer polder was reclaimed (1930). Drainage of the Northeast polder was completed in 1941. When a certain area was to be drained, a dike was built around the area. Afterwards, heavy diesel pumps were installed, which pumped the water out in one year. The island Urk was connected with the mainland this way, but it has always remained a fishing island. The engine power of its fleet is still the highest in Europe.

The Afsluitdijk

Once an area is drained, a muddy, impassable substance remains. In order to be able to cultivate the land, reed is sowed first. In a period of two years, the reed helps to evaporate the remaining water, it makes the ground receptive, and its roots help to make the ground firmer. After two years, the reed is burned down and the fields are prepared for cultivation by planting light crop that need no heavy machinery, such as rape. When it is blossoming in May and June, the rapefields are a beautiful sight (picture below). Later on, wheat is grown, and after five years, the ground has a firm upper layer of approximately 1,20 meter (4 feet). The result is a prosperous agricultural area that is leased to farmers, who grow potatoes, wheat and sugar beets. In the newly reclaimed polders, the State remains the owner of the land.

Bee-culture in the rape-seed fields.

Oostvaardersplassen, Nature Reserve

The Museum Nieuwland

Lelystad is the capital of the province of Flevoland, consisting totally of reclaimed land. The museum Nieuwland gives a good impression of the history of the development of this new area (picture below). Still, man gives nature something in return. The lowest part of the land, just behind the western dike, is designated a nature reserve (top picture).

Zeeland

In the province of Zeeland, the battle against the water has always been the hardest. The picture right shows the embankment of the river Oosterschelde, which is actually a sea-arm where the current used to flow at close distance along the dike. The dike had been frequently undermined and dissolved by this current. On the right of the upper picture is the Oosterschelde dike, which is backed up by another dike. In case the first dike subsided, the second one would protect the hinterland from the water. Because of the subsidements of the dikes, the village of Koudekerke disappeared. The only building remaining is the tower of the church. Since 1400, the southern coast of the island Schouwen-Duiveland has moved 4 kilometer (2.5 miles) inland.

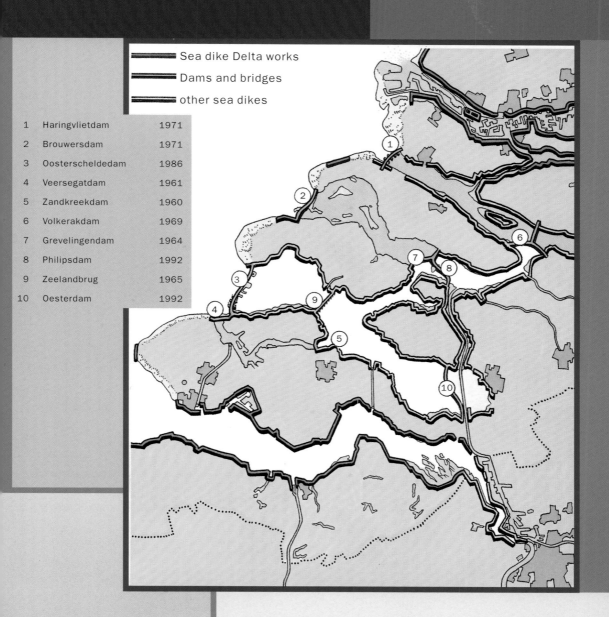

Sea dike Delta works

Dams and bridges

other sea dikes

The flooding of 1953 was the immediate cause for starting the Delta project. Most of the sea-arms were dammed, the first ones being the Zandkreek and the Veerse Gat, closed off in 1961. First, a dam was built at the rear-end of the island, as the tidal current was likely to damage the coast in this area. The most northern arm, Haringvliet, is currently a freshwater lake. The second one from the north, Grevelingen, is a salt-water lake. The third, the Oosterschelde, has an open connection with the sea via enormous doors in the dam, that can be closed during heavy weather.

The Flooding Disaster of 1953

The last great flood in Zeeland took place in the night of January 31st, 1953. A storm from the northwest had been driving the water in the direction of Zeeland for a few days. Combined with an exceptionally high tide, the dikes gave way at more than 200 places simultaneously. 1835 people lost their lives. The island Schouwen-Duiveland had turned into an inland sea. The largest breach was a few kilometers east of the tower on the previous page. It took until September of that same year to close the gap. Low and high tide had worn the gap until it was 520 meter (1700 feet) broad and 37 meter (121 feet) deep!

In order to fill the gap, concrete caissons were used. Because they are filled with air, caissons float on the water and are easily transported. Once they have reached their destination, the hatches in the bottom are opened and the caissons sink to their place. They still remain visible afterwards (picture right).

Delta Project

The inlet of the Oosterschelde is the breeding place to many fish. In order to safeguard the oyster and mussel farming, the Oosterschelde was to remain open, at least partially. Still, the hinterland had to be protected from the water as well. The most practical solution was to build a dam that would not disturb the water influx of the tides. The dam has a total of 62 doors, that can be closed during a storm surge. Three quarters of the normal difference in water level between low and high tide can thus be retained. Approximately twice a year, when the water level rises dangerously, the doors are shut. On the artificial island Neeltje Jans, where the concrete parts of the dam have been prepared, is an exhibition center that displays information about the dam in the Oosterschelde inlet.

Storm over the
Oosterschelde Dam

117

Square between the Abbey buildings

The City Hall

Middelburg

South of the great dams is Middelburg, the capital of Zeeland. Once upon a time, this was the biggest commercial town after Amsterdam. Many monuments have been kept, such as the city hall (picture below). Three generations of the Belgian family of architects Keldermans have worked on it between 1452 and 1520.

Of the guild houses, only the Kuiperspoort remains (picture right). In 1642, The guild of coopers ('kuipers') bought the gate building, located at the end of alley on the picture right, surrounded by warehouses. The doors placed at an angle with the wall are the doors to the basements of the warehouses. Currently, the complex is a school of music.

Around 1127 the abbey of Middelburg was founded by Premonstratensian monks. Until the reformation, it was the most powerful institution and the biggest landowner of Zeeland. Since 1574, the abbey is the seat of the provincial government. The picture far left at the top shows the former houses of the canons, currently the museum of Zeeland. The gate on the right is one of the oldest still visible remains of the abbey, dating from the beginning of the 13th century. The abbey is crowned with the 86.5 meter (283 feet) Long John, the bell tower of the former abbey churches, now both Protestant churches. It is visible from all over the island (picture below). The golden crown on the top of the tower is the crown of Count Willem II of Holland, Roman king of the German Empire, who generously provided the abbey with gifts (see also page 48) and is buried here.

's Hertogenbosch

's Hertogenbosch is the capital of the province of North Brabant, part of the old duchy Brabant, which had Brussels as its capital. The northern part of this duchy came under Dutch rule after the peace with Spain was signed. On the market square is the statue of painter Jeroen Bosch, who lived in 's Hertogenbosch around 1500.

the river Dieze in Uilenburg

King Philip II of Spain (p. 66) loved his absurdist images of hell. For this reason, Bosch's most beautiful paintings are in Madrid, in the Prado museum.

Until 1867, 's Hertogenbosch was a fortified city, and no one was allowed to build outside the city walls. Therefore, every square inch was used for construction, as the top picture shows. The houses were even built over the river Dieze.

Jeroen Bosch

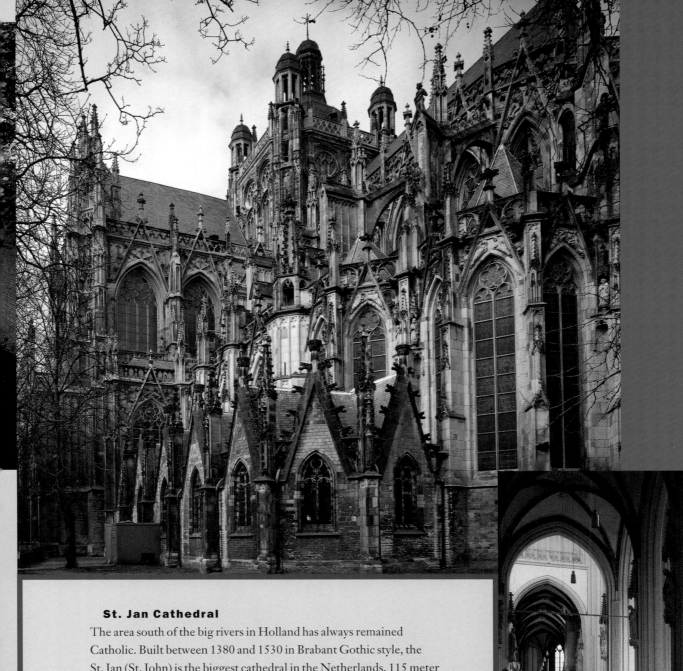

St. Jan Cathedral

The area south of the big rivers in Holland has always remained
Catholic. Built between 1380 and 1530 in Brabant Gothic style, the
St. Jan (St. John) is the biggest cathedral in the Netherlands, 115 meter
(377 feet) long. On the roof of the church, near the buttresses, are
personalized images of sins. There is a miser, frantically holding his
sack of money, a drunk, a bear eating from a pot of honey, and the devil
himself, accompanying the scene
with his flute. A total of 96 figures
sit on the buttresses.

121

Heusden

15 kilometer (9.5 miles) northwest of Den Bosch is the fortified town of Heusden. Built by the count of Holland to protect his land from his opponent, the duke of Brabant, some of the ramparts, as well as the authentic town center, are still intact. The old harbor on the river Maas has been restored in its original shape (picture left).

Eindhoven

Eindhoven, on the other hand, is a modern city with 197,000 inhabitants, making it the fifth largest city of the Netherlands. The Philips brothers founded their first light bulb factory here in 1891, which produced 500 bulbs a day (picture below). Nowadays, Philips is Europe's biggest electronics company, employing 30,000 people in Eindhoven alone.

Philips' first light bulb factory .

Oirschot

The landscape in the surroundings of Oirschot is dominated by forests and small fields marked by trees. The poplars form the raw material for making clogs, a highly developed industry in Brabant. Typical of Brabant are the small farms with green shutters, often built lengthwise alongside the roads (picture top left).

Some say Oirschot is the most picturesque village of Brabant. The center breaths tradition. On Tuesdays, the market square is a bustling place. The carillon of the 15th century church St. Pieter-in-de-Banden (St. Peter-in-the-bands) accompanies the market with a continuous waterfall of folk songs.

The old town hall of Oirschot

Maastricht

Deep in the south of the Netherlands is Maastricht (119,000 inhabitants), capital of the province of Limburg. In 1992, the treaty that laid the foundations of a united Europe without borders was established here, in the provincial government building (top picture).

St. Servaas Church

Maastricht's biggest square, Vrijthof, is dominated by the Romanesque St. Servaas Church (picture top middle). Saint Servaas was the first bishop of Maastricht. Legend has it that the apostle St. Peter personally handed him the key to the gate of heaven. Just left of the St. Servaas is the Protestant St. Jan (St. John's) Church, built in the 15th century as the parish church of the common people. The bell tower is inspired by that of the cathedral of Utrecht (p. 68). The gray building on the right of the church is the main guard house, dating from 1736.

Terrace on the Vrijthof

Petrus Mickelers

Many 17th and 18th-century houses have extremely high attics, dating from the days that Maastricht was still a fortified city. The building of a house was only permitted if the owner was willing to create enough space for a food-depository. In this way, the city was able to withstand a siege of three months. The statue at the bottom resembles the monk Petrus Minckelers, who invented the technique of generating gas from coal by the end of the 18th century.

Vrijthof with St. Servaas and St.Jan

The City Hall

The 1664 city hall is built in Dutch Classicist style. Officially Maastricht had two masters, namely the States of Holland, owning the right half of the city and the Bishop of Liege, owning the left half. The perfect symmetry of the building expresses the equivalence of both masters.

House on the river Jeker

The picture left shows the typical architectural style of 'Maasland', the area around Maastricht. The combination of limestone and bricks in architecture, echoing the style of German and English half-timbered houses from those days, was forbidden from the 17th century onwards, because it increased the danger of fire.

St. Servaas Bridge

The St. Servaas bridge, dating from 1298, is the oldest bridge in the Netherlands, it replaces an even older bridge that had collapsed when a procession of 400 people crossed it. To avoid further disasters, a more solid stone bridge was built.

Maastricht has always been of major strategic importance. When Louis XIV (the Sun King) conquered the city in 1673, one of the three musketeers, d' Artagnan, lost his life. The military museum of the Dome des Invalides in Paris has a scale-model of 18th century Maastricht, made by the French secret service. The Bonnefanten Museum in Maastricht owns a copy.

St. Servaas Bridge

Hellepoort

In 1229, Duke Hendrik I of Brabant granted permission for the construction of the first city ramparts; one of which, the Hellepoort (Hell's Gate, picture right), remains to date. On some of these ramparts, houses were built in later centuries. The ancient breast work is currently a footpath (picture top middle).

Hellepoort

127

Eating and Drinking

Dutch cuisine is known in particular for its winter dishes, such as pea soup and kale. The Dutch are also very proud of their beefsteak, although for people who prefer their steak well-done it may take some getting used to, as a proper Dutch steak should be red inside.

Pea-Soup

Ingredients (4 persons):

1 pound of green peas
5 pints of water
3 ounces of fresh bacon
1 pound of Dutch smoked sausage
1 pig's trotter
1.5 pounds of potatoes
2 bunches of celery
1.5 pounds of leek
1 celeriac
1 ounce of salt

Wash the peas and soak them in the water. Boil the meat and the bacon, along with the peas, for two hours.

Add the peeled and cut potatoes for the last half hour.

Remove the peas and the potatoes from the broth, stir them to a pulp and strain. Mix the pulp with the simmering water again and add the cut vegetables, sausage and salt. Boil for half an hour, or until the meat and vegetables are cooked.

Remove the meat, slice, and put it back in. Cut the celery and add to the soup. Your soup is ready now; make sure you do not boil it any longer.

The soup tastes even nicer when you reheat it the next day.

Pea soup, like kale, is mostly eaten on cold winter days.

Kale
with sausage

Ingredients (4 persons):
2 pounds of kale
3 pounds of potatoes
salt
1 pound of Dutch smoked sausage
boiled milk
4 ounces of smoked bacon

Remove the hard parts of the kale and
wash it. Boil the kale, together with the
bacon and salt for fifteen minutes in
water. Add the peeled potatoes, as well as
some water, and cook for half an hour.
Remove the bacon, mash the rest and stir
the milk through. Wash the sausage and
heat it up in water, but do not boil. Leave
the
sausage in the water for half an hour, to
prevent the skin from breaking, and slice
before serving.

Pancakes

Children love pancakes,
and they are easy to make

Ingredients (4 persons):
5 ounces of flour
2 eggs
1 pint of milk
2 drams of salt
2 ounces of butter

Stir the flour, 2 eggs and 150 ml milk to a
smooth batter. Dilute the batter with the
rest of the milk while stirring.
Melt some butter in a pan and add the
batter until the bottom of the pan is just
covered. Bake the pancake so fast, that
the bottom side is done when the batter
has dried. Now turn the pancake. If you
are not as skilful as the cook on the picture, use a spatula. The top side should now
be brown. After baking the other side,
remove the pancake and pile up the
pancakes on a plate. Cover the pancakes
with another plate to keep warm, and
serve with sugar, syrup or jam. Your
children will love it!

Fun on the ice

Usually, winters in Holland are mild, mostly
accompanied by wind and rain. Still, although it
does not last very long, most years do have a frost
period. At this point, nearly everybody goes onto
the ice. In the 17th century, things were very much
the same. The painting by Hendrick Avercamp in
the Museum Mauritshuis (p. 48) gives a good
impression of fun on the ice. But there are risks to it
as well. On the left of the painting, three people
have fallen through the ice...

Fun on the ice, Hendrik Avercamp

A Short History of the Netherlands

Middle Ages

In the Middle Ages, the Netherlands were a part of the German Empire, also known as the Holy Roman Empire. The area was rather isolated. Thus local noblemen, like the counts of Holland, could obtain a high amount of freedom. One of them, Willem II, even became King of the Roman Empire (p. 48; 119). After the death of the last count of Holland, the county fell into the hands of the Wittelbachs from Bavaria, Germany. Afterwards, the dukes of Burgundy (p. 64)

15th century

became their successors. During the 15th century, the entire area of Holland, Belgium, Luxembourg and large parts of northern France were united under their rule. From the 14th century onward, Amsterdam developed into an important harbor. Traders imported wheat and amber from the Baltic area, wool from Great Britain and wine and salt from France. After the discovery of the new continents, Spanish and Portuguese harbors supplied Amsterdam with spices.

The last heiress of Burgundy, Maria the Rich, married the Habsburg emperor Maximilian of Austria (p.26). Their only son, Philip the Fair, married Castilian Joan the Insane . Their son, Charles V (p.83), became both king of Spain and ruler of the Burgundian empire. Thus, Holland came under Spanish rule. At the same time, Protestantism came to the Netherlands. During the rule of Charles' son Philip II, the Eighty Years' War of Independence broke out. The first Dutch leader was William of Orange (p. 57, 67). Philip

1573

II sent one of his most experienced generals, the Duke of Alva, to the Netherlands, but from 1573 the tide began to turn in favor of the Dutch. The Spanish army was forced to give up the siege of Alkmaar (p.77), and the Spanish fleet was defeated and destroyed near Hoorn (p.78).

1585

Initially, the war seemed to threaten the rising Dutch trade. However, the conquest of Antwerp in 1585 by the Spanish brought many refugees to Amsterdam. Trade moved from Antwerp to Middelburg (p.118), and especially to Amsterdam. As the Spanish and

1602
1621

Portuguese harbors remained closed for the Dutch during the war, they were forced to explore new areas themselves. The world's first public limited company, the Dutch East

India Company (p.16), was founded in 1602. Shortly afterwards, in 1621, the West India Company, responsible for the colonization of America, was founded. The West India Company founded the city of New Amsterdam, which was later sold to the English and renamed New York. For a short period, the company even had colonies in present day Brazil (p. 48).

The war with Spain came to an end only with the 1648 peace-treaty of Münster, Germany. The same treaty ended the Thirty Years' German War. This treaty saw the official partition of Holland from the German Empire. The War of the Spanish Succession ended in 1713 with the treaty of Utrecht. In the 17th and 18th centuries, the Netherlands were a federal republic, ruled mainly by the trading cities. The members of the Dutch Royal Family are the descendants of the 17th-century stadtholders or provincial governors. In the meantime, the Dutch strength as a trading nation had declined somewhat. Around 1700, Amsterdam lost its position as the major harbor to London, but remained the financial center of the world.

1648
1713

After the Napoleonic age, during the congress of Vienna in 1813, it was decided that the Netherlands were to become a monarchy, consisting of Belgium, Luxembourg and the Netherlands. Shortly afterwards, in 1830, Belgium separated from Holland. Luxembourg kept its ties with the Netherlands in a personal union: the king of the Netherlands was, until 1890, the grand duke of Luxembourg.

1813
1830

Economically, the Netherlands was a somewhat backward country in the previous century. The German writer Heinrich Heine once wrote: 'When the end of the world approaches I'll move to Holland, because everything happens there fifty years later'. Industrialization did not reach Holland until 1890 (p.122). Rotterdam developed into the main harbor for the German industrial area and has been the biggest harbor in the world since 1940-centuries after Amsterdam held that position. In that sense, Holland is back in its old role, 300 years later.

1890
1940

Geographical data:

Surface:	41,526 km² (16,033 square miles)
consisting of:	33,889 km² (13,085 square miles) of land
	7,637 km² (2,949 square miles) of water

Highest point:	321 meter (1053 feet) above average sea level at high tide
Lowest point:	6.9 meter (22 feet, 8 inches) below average sea level at high tide

Weather (Source: De Bilt, near Utrecht):

Annual rainfall: 820 mm (32 inches)

Temperature:	winter	spring	summer	autumn
day:	5.3 C (41.5 F)	12.8 C (55 F)	21.0 C (69.8 F)	15.8 C (60.4 F)
night:	-0.2 C (31.6 F)	3.9 C (39.2 F)	11.2 C (52.2 F)	6.3 C (43.3 F)

Population

Number of inhabitants:	15.5 million
Number of cows:	4.4 million
Number of pigs:	13.2 million
Number of sheep:	1.6 million
Number of chickens:	91 million

Population density: 457 inhabitants per square kilometer (1184 inhabitants per square mile)

Religion

Catholic:	33%
Protestant and Reformed:	21%
Other Religions:	7%
Not religious:	40%

The five largest cities:

1. Amsterdam   718,000
2. Rotterdam   593,000
3. The Hague   443,000
4. Utrecht   234,000
5. Eindhoven   197,000

Labor force

Average income
Net monthly income:	ƒ 2,731,-
Gross monthly income:	ƒ 4,237,-

21% of this income is spent on rent.
Percentage of rented houses: 52%

Life expectancy:

Male:	75 years
Female:	80 years

Average length and weight:

Male:	1.79 meter (5 feet, 10 inches)	79.0 kilo (174 pounds)
Female:	1.67 meter (5 feet, 6 inches)	66.6 kilo (147 pounds)

Some data on consumption:

Beer consumption:	86 liter (23 gallons)
Softdrink consumption:	97 liter (26 gallons)
Wine (including Sherry, Port):	17 liter (4 gallons)

GENERAL INFORMATION

Business hours of shops

Monday to Friday from 9 am to 6 pm; supermarkets often from 9 am to 8 pm. On Monday mornings, many shops are closed. In big cities, shops often do not open till 10 am, in smaller cities and villages, shops sometimes close between 12:30 and 2 pm.

Bigger cities have late night shopping once a week; shops stay open till 9 pm. In Amsterdam and The Hague, late opening is on Thursday, in Rotterdam and Delft on Friday.

Shops are closed on Sundays, although in Rotterdam and The Hague they open the first Sunday of the month. In Amsterdam, some shops, such as the Bijenkorf department store, open every Sunday from noon to 5 pm, others open several Sundays of the month.

Car Traffic

Maximum speed:
In built-up areas: 50 km per hour (31 miles per hour)
Outside built-up areas: 80 km per hour (50 miles per hour)
On the motorway: 120 km per hour (75 miles per hour), unless otherwise indicated.
Near big cities there is often a speed limit of 100 km per hour (62 miles per hour).

In practically all city centers there are fees for parking. In some municipalities, traffic wardens are very quick to attach wheel clamps.

Telephone Cards

Most telephone booths nowadays operate with telephone cards. German telephone cards are valid in the Netherlands and vice versa.

Telephone cards can be purchased at post offices, the official GWK exchange offices, tobacco shops and the VVV, the official tourist offices.

Public Transport

Public transport in the Netherlands operates on workdays from 6 am to midnight, on Saturdays from 7 am to midnight, and on Sundays from 8 am to midnight. Night buses and trains operate in and between big cities.

Single tickets can be bought on trams and buses, but if you use public transport more frequently, a 'strippenkaart' comes in handy if you use public transport 4 times or more it is cheaper than paying for single tickets all the time. A strippenkaart contains 15 strips. Every time you travel, you must stamp a certain amount of strips, depending on the length of your trip. For this purpose, a city or a district is divided into zones. If you travel within one zone, you must stamp two strips. If your destination lies beyond the present zone, you must count the amount of zones that you travel through, add one and stamp accordingly. There is also the possibility of buying a day, week, or month ticket for a certain amount of zones. Strippenkaarten can be bought at most tourist offices, post offices, tobacco shops and bus or train stations.

GWK Exchange Offices

The official exchange office GWK has a large knowledge of foreign currencies and has a history of helping foreign visitors. GWK-offices are open seven days a week from early in the morning till late at night. They are located at 35 train stations, Schiphol Airport, and the border crossings with Germany and Belgium.

The GWK-offices change most foreign currencies, both western and non-western, as well as traveller's cheques. For insurances or Cash Advances for creditcard holders (Eurocard, Access, Master Card, Diners Card, Visa Card) you can go here. The GWK-office can offer several excursions and tickets for attractions, such as the Rijksmuseum, canaltrips and several amusement parks. The Western Union Money Transfer service offered here enables you to send money to and from more than 70 countries in the world within minutes.

At the GWK-office in the Central Station of Amsterdam (open 24 hours a day, 7 days a week) you can make reservations for a variety of hotel rooms at good rates. Other GWK-offices in Amsterdam include the Amstel station branch and the Sloterdijk branch.

AMSTERDAM

Tourist Offices (VVV)

The VVV (= Association for foreign traffic) is the official tourist office of the Netherlands. The VVV provides information about tourism, culture and recreation. The VVV can provide you with information about: hotel reservations; excursions; roundtrips (also by boat); maps and guides; walking routes; tickets for public transport, theater, concerts; souvenirs; telephone cards; posters; VVV-gift vouchers; money exchange. VVV Amsterdam has four branches:

Central station.
Opening hours: daily from 7:45 am to 8 pm.

Opposite the central station.
Opening hours: daily from 9 am to 5 pm.

Corner Leidseplein/Leidsestraat:
Opening hours: daily from 9 am to 8 pm., Sundays until 5.

Stadionplein
(corner Van Tuyl van Serooskerkenweg).
Daily from 9 am to 5 pm. Closed on Sundays.

At Schiphol airport,
tourist services are provided at Holland Tourist Information at Schiphol Plaza, open daily from 7 am to 10 pm.

VVV can be reached by telephone from Monday to Friday from 9 am to 5 pm.; tel. number: 0900-4004040 (f 1 per minute).

page 8
Royal Palace (Koninklijk Paleis)
Nieuwezijds Voorburgwal 147
1012 RJ Amsterdam
tel: 020 - 6248698

Opening hours:
From approximately 12:30 pm to 4/5 pm.
Closed from 1 to 18 January
from 25 to 30 April
from 1 to 16 and 20 to 31 May
from 13 to 17 June
from 23 to 26 June
from 8 to 12 September
from 6 to 30 September
from 1 to 10 October
from 27 to 28 October

Admission fees:
Children until 4: free
Children until 12: f 1.50
CYP holders/city pass holders/pass 65+ holders /students: f 3
Adults: f 5

page 8
New Church (Nieuwe Kerk)
Dam / Gravenstraat 17
1012 NL Amsterdam
tel: 020 - 6386909

Opening hours:
11 am to 5 pm.
Precise opening hours, opening days and admission fees depend on the expositions.

page 10
Amsterdam Historic Museum (Amsterdams Historisch Museum)
Kalverstraat 92/Nieuwezijds Voorburgwal 357.
1012 RM Amsterdam
tel: 020 - 5231822

Opening hours:
Monday to Friday: 10 am to 5 pm.
Saturday and Sunday: 11 am to 5 pm.

Admission fees:
Children until 6: free
Children until 16: f 4.50
Adults: f 9
65+: f 6.75
CYP holders: f 6.75
Annual season museum ticket holders: free
Admission to the militia's gallery is free.

page 16
Dutch Maritime Museum (Nederlands Scheepvaart Museum)
Kattenburgerplein 1
1018 KK Amsterdam
020 - 5232311

Opening hours:
Tuesday to Saturday: 10 am to 5 pm. Sundays and national holidays: noon to 5 pm.
Closed on New Year's Day and Queen's Day (30th of April).
Also open on Mondays from mid-June to mid-September.

Admission fees:
Children until 5: free
Children until 17: f 8
Adults: f 12.50
65+: f 10
CYP holders until 17: f 6.50
CYP holders 18+: f 10
Annual season museum ticket holders: free

page 19
Museum Van Loon
Keizersgracht 672
1017 ET Amsterdam
tel: 020 - 6245255

Opening hours:
Sunday: 1 to 5 pm.
Monday: 11 am to 5 pm.
Tuesday: 11 am to 5 pm.
Children until 13: free
Adults: ƒ 7.50
65+: ƒ 5

page 23
Our Lord in the Attic (Onze Lieve Heer op Solder)
Oudezijds Voorburgwal 44
1012 GE Amsterdam
tel: 020 - 6246604

Opening hours:
Monday to Saturday:
10 am to 5 pm.
Sundays and national holidays:
1 to 5 pm.
Closed on 1 January and 30 April.

Admission fees:
Children until 4: free
Children until 18: ƒ 5
Adults: ƒ 7.50
CYP holders and students: ƒ 5
65+: ƒ 5
Annual season museum ticket
holders: free

page 28
Anne Frank House (Anne Frank Huis)
Prinsengracht 263
1016 GV Amsterdam
tel: 020 - 6667100

Opening hours:
1 April to 31 August:
Monday to Saturday: 9 am to 7 pm.
Sunday: 10 am to 7 pm
1 September to 31 March:
Monday to Saturday: 9 am to 5 pm.
Sunday: 10 am to 5 pm.
Closed on 1 January, 25 December
and 'Day of Atonement'.

Admission fees:
Children until 10: free
Children until 17/CYP holders: ƒ 5
Adults: ƒ 10
65+: ƒ 7.50

page 30
Portuguese Synagogue (Portugees-Israelitische Synagoge)
Mr. Visscherplein 3,
1011 RD Amsterdam
tel: 020 - 6245351

Opening hours:
1 April to 31 October:
Sunday to Friday: 10 am to 12:30
pm, and 1 pm to 4 pm.
1 November to 31 March:
Monday to Thursday: 10 am to
12:30 pm, and 1 pm to 4 pm.
Friday: 10 am to 12:30 pm, and 1
pm to 3 pm.
Sunday: 10 am to 12 pm.

Admission fees:
Children from 12 till 18: ƒ 2.50
Adults: ƒ 5

Closed on Jewish holidays

page 31
Diamond Cutteries
In 1982, 5 leading diamond
cutteries in Amsterdam decided to
form the Diamond Foundation
Amsterdam (DFA). The five
partners of the Diamond
Foundation Amsterdam are open 7
days a week. When you enter, you
can see the diamond cutters
working. During the one-hour
tour, a guide tells you where
diamonds are found, how they are
cut and how their quality is
determined. In the showrooms,
diamonds of several qualities and
shapes are displayed, and especially
differences in color can be be
noted. A large collection of loose
cut diamonds is present, as well as

an extensive collection of jewels.

Opening hours:
10 am to 5 pm.
Admission: free

Addresses:

Gassan Diamonds B.V.
Nieuwe Uilenburgerstraat 173-175
1011 LN Amsterdam
tel: 020 - 6225333

Coster Diamonds
Paulus Potterstraat 2-6
1071 CZ Amsterdam
tel: 020 - 6762222

Van Moppes Diamonds
Albert Cuypstraat 2-6
1072 CT Amsterdam
tel: 020 - 6761242

Holshuijsen-Stoeltie
Wagenstraat 13-17
1017 CZ Amsterdam
tel: 020 - 6237601

Amsterdam Diamond Center
Rokin 1-5
1012 KK Amsterdam
tel: 020 - 6245787

page 40
National Museum (Rijksmuseum)
Stadhouderskade 42
1071 ZD Amsterdam
tel: 020 - 6732121
General information: 06 - 8898

Opening hours:
daily from 10 am to 5 pm.
Closed on 1 January.

Admission fees:
Children until 18: ƒ 5
Adults: ƒ 12.50
65+: ƒ 7.50

page 42

Rijksmuseum Vincent van Gogh

Paulus Potterstraat 7
1071 CX Amsterdam
tel: 020 - 5705200

Opening hours:
daily from 10 am to 5 pm.
Closed on 1 January.

Admission fees:
Children until 5: free
Children until 18/CYP holders: *f* 5
Adults: *f* 12.50
Annual season museum ticket holders: free

page 45

Amsterdam ArenA

Haaksbergweg 59
1101 BR Amsterdam-Zuidoost
tel: 020 - 3111333

Opening hours:
Daily tours (approximately 1.5 hours).
Reservation necessary

Admission fees:
Children until 12: *f* 12.50
Adults: *f* 15.00

ZAANDAM

Tourist office (VVV)

Gedempte Gracht 76
1506 CJ Zaandam
tel: 075 - 6162221

page 46

Paint mill de Kat (Verfmolen de Kat)

Kalverringdijk 29
1509 BT Zaandam
tel: 075 - 6210477

Opening hours:
From April to October:
Tuesday to Sunday: 9 am to 5 pm.

From November to March:
Saturday and Sunday:
9 am to 5 pm.
Easter Monday, Whit Monday and Mondays in July and August:
9 am to 5 pm.

Admission fees:
Children until 3: free
Children until 14: *f* 1.50
Adults: *f* 3.50

page 46

Oil mill de Zoeker (Oliemolen de Zoeker)

Kalverringdijk 31
1509 BT Zaandam
tel: 075 - 6287942

Opening hours:
From 15 March to 1 October:
Sunday to Friday:
9:30 am to 4:30 pm.
From 1 July to 31 August:
Also on Saturdays: 9:30 am to 4:30.

Admission fees:
Children until 3: free
children until 15: *f* 1,50.
Adults: *f* 3.50

page 47

Museum shop Albert Heijn

Kalverringdijk 5
1509 BT Zaandam
tel: 075 - 6169619

Opening hours:
From 1 March to 1 November:
daily: 10 am to noon,
and 1 pm to 5 pm.
From 1 November to 1 March:
Saturday and Sunday: 11 am to 1 pm and 2 pm to 4 pm.
A maximum of 10 persons at a time can visit the shop.

Admission free

Page 47

Czar Peter's House (Czar Peterhuisje)

Krimp 23
1506 AA Zaandam
tel: 075 - 6160390

Opening hours:
From April to October:
Tuesday to Friday:
10 am to 1 am, and 2 pm to 5 pm.
Throughout the year:
Saturday and Sunday: 1 pm to 5 pm.

Admission fees:
Children: *f* 1.50
Adults: *f* 2.50
Annual season museum ticket holders: free

THE HAGUE

Tourist Office (vvv)

Nassaulaan 25
2514 JT Den Haag
tel: 06 - 340305051
070 - 3617915

page 48

Foundation Visitors Center Binnenhof (Stichting Bezoekers-centrum Binnenhof)

Binnenhof 8A
2513 AA Den Haag
070 - 3646144

Opening hours:
Monday to Saturday:
10 am to 3:45 pm.

Admission fees:
Children until 12: *f* 5
Adults: *f* 6
65+: *f* 5

page 48
Museum Mauritshuis
Korte Vijverberg 8
2513 AB Den Haag
tel: 070 - 3023456

Opening hours:
Tuesday to Saturday:
10 am to 5 pm.
Sunday: 11 am to 5 pm.
Closed on Monday.

Admission fees:
Children until 17 jaar/CYP
holders: ƒ 5
Adults: ƒ 10
Annual season museum ticket
holders: free

page 51
Peace Palace
(Vredespaleis)
Carnegieplein 2
2628 AR Den Haag
tel: 070 - 3024242

Guided tours (with reservation):
From 1 May to 1 October:
Monday to Friday: at 10 am, 11 am,
2 pm, 3 pm and at 4 pm.
From 1 October to 1 May: at 10
am, 11 am, 2 pm and at 3 pm.

Admission fees:
Children until 12: ƒ 3
Adults: ƒ 5

page 52
Panorama Mesdag
Zeestraat 65
2518 AA Den Haag
tel: 070 - 3106665

Opening hours:
Monday to Saturday:
10 am to 5 pm.
Sundays and holidays:
noon to 5 pm.
Closed on 25 December.

page 54
Madurodam
George Maduroplein 1
2584 RZ Den Haag
tel: 070 - 3553900

Opening hours:
From 1 January to 23 March:
9 am to 5 pm.
From 24 March to 30 September:
9 am to 10 pm.
From 1 October to 31 December:
9 am to 5 pm.

Admission fees:
Children upto 3: free
Children upto 11: ƒ 14
Adults: ƒ 19,50
60+: ƒ 16

APELDOORN

page 55
Palace Het Loo
(Paleis Het Loo)
Koninklijk Park 1
7315 JA Apeldoorn
tel: 055-5772400

Opening hours:
Tuesday to Sunday:
10 am to 5 pm.
Closed on Mondays, except on
holidays.
Closed on 25 December.

Admission fees:
Children until 5: free
Children until 17: ƒ 10
Adults: ƒ 12,50
65+: ƒ 10
Annual season museum ticket
holders: free

DELFT

Tourist office (VVV)
Markt 83-85
2611 GS Delft
tel: 015 - 2126100

page 57
New Church
(Nieuwe Kerk)
Markt 2
2611 GT Delft
tel: 015 - 2123025

Opening hours:
From 17 March to 1 November:
9 am to 6 pm.
From 2 November to 16 March:
11 am to 4 pm.

**Admission Nieuwe Kerk or
climbing the bell tower:**
Children until 12: ƒ 1.50
Adults: ƒ 3.25
65+: ƒ 3

**Nieuwe Kerk in combination
with Old Church (Oude Kerk)**
Children until 12: ƒ 1.50
Adults: ƒ 2.25
65+: ƒ 1.50

page 57
Delft Ware Factories:

De Candelaer
Kerkstraat 14
2611 GX Delft
tel: 015 - 2131848

Opening hours:
From March to December:
Monday to Saturday:
8:30 am to 6 pm.
Sunday: 8:30 am to 5 pm.
January and February:
Monday to Saturday:
8:30 am to 6 pm.
Closed on Sundays

Admission free

Earthenware Factory de Delftse Pauw
Delftweg 133
2289 BD Rijswijk
tel: 015 - 2124920

Opening hours:
From 1 April to 15 October:
Daily from 9 am to 4:30 pm.
From 16 October to 31 March:
Monday to Friday:
9 am to 4:30 pm.
Saturday and Sunday:
11 am to 1 pm.

Admission free

N.V. Koninklijke Delftsch Earthenware Factory
De Porceleyne Fles Anno 1653
Rotterdamse Weg 196
2628 AR Delft
tel: 015 - 2569214

Opening hours:
From 1 April to 31 October:
Monday to Saturday: 9 am to 5 pm.
Sundays and holidays:
9:30 am to 5 pm.

Admission: f 5

page 58
Prinsenhof
Sint Agathaplein 1
2611 HR Delft
tel: 015 - 2602358

Opening hours:
Tuesday to Saturday: 10 am to 5 pm.
Sundays and holidays:
1 pm to 5 pm. Closed on 31
December and 1 January.

Admission fees:
Children until 12: free
Children until 16: f 2.50
Adults: f 5.00
65+: f 2,50
Annual season museum ticket holders: free

ROTTERDAM

Tourist Information (VVV)
Coolsingel 67
3012 AC Rotterdam
tel: 0900 - 4034065 (f 0.50 per minute)

page 60
Tours around the harbor:
Havenrondvaarten SPIDO
Leuvehoofd 5 (follow signs:
Havens 172-174)
3011 XT Rotterdam
tel: 010 - 4135400

The boats leave
from April to September:
9:30 am to 5 pm. Boarding every 45
minutes for a roundtrip of
75 minutes. Supplementary
information on request.

Admission fees:
Children until 2: free.
Children until 11: f 7.50
Adults: f 15

Page 61
Panorama Tower Euromast
Parkhaven 20
3016 GM Rotterdam
tel: 010 - 4364811

Opening hours:
From April to September:
Daily from 10 am to 7 pm.
From July to August:
Sunday and Monday:
10 am to 7 pm.
Tuesday to Saturday:
10 am to 10:30 pm.

Admission fees:
Children until 3: free
Children until: 12: f 9
Adults: f 14.50

Page 62
Show-Cube (Kijkkubus)
Overblaak 70
3011 MH Rotterdam
tel: 010 - 4142285

Opening hours:
January and February:
Friday, Saturday and Sunday:
11 am to 5 pm.
March, April, May, October,
November and December:
Tuesday to Friday: 10 am to 5 pm.
Saturday and Sunday: 11 am to 5 pm.
From June to September:
Monday to Friday: 10 am to 5 pm.
Saturday and Sunday: 11 am to 5 pm.

Admission fees:
Children until 3: free
Children until 12: f 2.50
Adults: f 3.50
65+: f 2.50

GOUDA

Tourist Information (VVV)
Markt 27
2801 JJ Gouda
tel: 0182 - 513666

Page 64
City Hall (Stadhuis)
Markt 1
2801 JG Gouda
tel: 0128 - 588758

Opening hours:
Monday to Friday: 9 am to 11 am.
Saturday: 11 am to 1 pm.

Admission fee: f 1,-

St. John's Church (Sint-Jan)
Achter de Kerk 2
2801 JW Gouda
tel: 0182 - 5121684

Opening hours:
From March to October:
Monday to Saturday: 9 am to 5 pm.
From November to February:
Monday to Saturday:
10 am to 4 pm.
Closed on Sundays

Admission fees:
Children until 3: free
Children until 12: ƒ 1
Children until 17: ƒ 1.50
Adults: ƒ 3
CYP holders: ƒ 2
65+: ƒ 2

UTRECHT

Tourist Information (VVV) Utrecht
Vredenburg 90
3501 DC Utrecht
tel: 030 - 2331544

Cathedral (Dom)
Achter de Dom 1
3512 JH Utrecht
tel: 030 - 2310403

Opening hours:
Monday to Friday: 10 am to 5 pm.
Saturday: 10 am to 3:30 pm.
Sunday: 2 pm to 4 pm.

NAARDEN

Tourist Information (VVV) Gooi- en Vechtstreek
Adriaan Dortsmanplein 1B
1411 RC Naarden
tel: 035 - 6942836

Dutch Fortress Museum (Nederlands Vestingmuseum)
Westwalstraat 6
1411 PB Naarden
tel: 035 - 6945459

Opening hours:
The weekend before Easter until
31 October and the Christmas
holidays:
Monday to Friday:
10:30 am to 5 pm.
Saturday, Sunday and holidays:
noon to 5 pm.
From 1 November to the weekend
before Easter:
Saturday and Sunday, 26
December en 1 January:
noon to 4 pm.

Admission fees:
Children until 3: free
Children until 11: ƒ 5
Adults: ƒ 7.50
65+: ƒ 6
Annual season museum ticket
holders: free

City Hall Naarden (Stadhuis Naarden)
Marktstraat 22
1411 EA Naarden
tel: 035 - 6957811

Opening hours:
Monday to Saturday: 1:30 pm to
4:30 pm. The city hall is open to
the public when no meetings,
weddings, etc. are taking place.

St. Vitus Church (St.-Vituskerk)
Sint-Annastraat 5
(entrance: Marktstraat)
1411 PE Naarden
tel: 035 - 6949873

Opening hours:
May and June (depending on the
photo festival which takes place
every two years) until second
Sunday of September:
Daily from 2 to 4 pm.
Saturdays: 3:45 to 4:15 pm. Tours
are accompanied by organ music.

Comenius museum
Kloosterstraat 33
1411 RS Naarden

Opening hours:
From 1 April to 31 October:
Tuesday to Saturday:
10 am to 5 pm.
Sundays and holidays:
noon to 5 pm.
1 November to 31 March:
Tuesday to Sundays and holidays:
1 to 4 pm.
Closed on 25 December,
31 December en 1 January.

Admission fees:
Children until 5: free
Children until 12: ƒ 1.50
Adults: ƒ 3.50
CYP holders/65+ pass: ƒ 1.50
Annual season museum ticket
holders: free

HAARLEM

Tourist Information (VVV)
Stationsplein 1
2011 LR Haarlem
tel: 0900 - 6161600

page 74
St. Bavo Church
(Grote- of St.-Bavokerk)
Oude Groenmarkt 23
2011 HL Haarlem
tel: 023 - 5324399

page 74
Meat Hall (Vleeshal)
Grote Markt 16
2011 RD Haarlem
tel : 023 - 51642000

Opening hours:
Monday to Saturday:
11 am to 5 pm.
Sundays and holidays:
1 pm to 5 pm.
Closed on 25 December and
1 January.

Admission fees:
Children until 9: free
Children until 17: *f* 2.50
Adults: *f* 4
65+: *f* 2.50

page 75
Frans-Halsmuseum
Groot Heiligland 62
2011 ES Haarlem
tel: 023 - 5319180

Opening hours:
Monday to Saturday:
11 am to 5 pm.
Sundays and holidays: 1 to 5 pm.
Closed on 25 December en
1 January.

Admission fees:
Children until 9: free.
Children until 17: *f* 3.50
Adults: *f* 7.50
65+: *f* 3.50

ALKMAAR

Tourist Information
(VVV) Alkmaar and
surroundings:
Waagplein 3
1811 JP Alkmaar
tel: 072 - 5114284

page 76
Dutch Cheese Museum
(Hollands Kaasmuseum)
Waagplein 2
1811 JP Alkmaar
tel: 072 - 5114284

Opening hours:
Monday to Saturday: 1
0 am to 4 pm.
Closed on Sundays.
Admission fees:
Children until 2: free
Over 2 years old, adults: *f* 3
Annual season museum ticket
holders: free

HOORN

Tourist Information
(VVV) Region
Westfriesland
Veemarkt 4
1621 JC Hoorn
tel: 0900 - 4031055

page 79
West Frisian Museum
(Westfries Museum)
Rode Steen 1
1621 CV Hoorn
tel: 0229 - 290028

Opening hours:
Monday to Friday: 11 am to 5 pm.
Saturday and Sundays: 2 to 5 pm.
Sundays from 30 March to 28
September: noon to 5 pm.

Admission fees:
Children until 16: *f* 2.50
Adults: *f* 5
65+: *f* 2.50
Annual season museum ticket
holders: free

ENKHUIZEN

Tourist Information
(VVV) Region
Westfriesland
Tussen Twee Havens 1
1601 EM Enkhuizen
tel: 0228 - 313164

page 80
Zuiderzeemuseum
Wierdijk 42
(large parking area with ferry at the
beginning of the dike Lelystad-
Enhuizen)
1601 LA Enkhuizen
tel: 0228 - 318260

Opening hours:
April to October:
daily from 10 am to 5 pm.
July and August:
daily from 10 am to 7 pm.
From November to March, the
open-air part is closed.

Admission fees:
Children until 3: free.
Children until 12: *f* 10
Adults: *f* 15
65+: *f* 12
Annual season museum ticket
holders: free

EDAM

Tourist Information
(VVV) Edam
Damplein 1
1135 BK Edam
tel: 0299 - 371717

Edams Museum
Damplein 8
1135 BK Edam
tel: 0299 - 372644

Opening hours:
From Good Friday to the end of
October:
Tuesday to Saturday:
10 am to 4:30 pm.
Sunday: 1:30 pm to 4:30 pm.

Admission fees:
Children until 3: free
Children until 14: ƒ 1.50
Adults: ƒ 3
65+: ƒ 1.50
Annual season museum ticket
holders: free

TULIP FIELDS

Keukenhof
Stationsweg 166A
2161 AM Lisse
tel: 0252 - 465555

Opening hours in 1998:
26 March to 24 May: daily from 8
am to 7:30 pm. Ticket office open
till 6 pm.

Admission fees:
Children: ƒ 8.50
Adults: ƒ 17.50

AALSMEER

Flower Auction
Legmeerdijk 313
1431 GB Aalsmeer
tel: 0297 - 392185

Opening hours:
Monday to Friday: 7:30 to 11 am.

Admission fees:
Children until 11: free
Adults: ƒ 5

KINDERDIJK:

Visitor's Mill Kinderdijk
Nederwaard 5
2961 AS Kinderdijk
tel: 078 - 6915179

Opening hours:
1 April to 30 September:
Monday to Saturday: 9:30 am to
5:30 pm.
Sunday: 9:30 am to 5 pm.

Admission fees (except on
Saturday afternoons in July and
August):
Children until 3: free
Children until 15: ƒ 1.75
Adults: ƒ 3

On Saturday afternoons in July and
August, the entire windmill area is
open to the public. Admission fees
on Saturday afternoons after
1 o'clock in July en August:
Children from 4 to 15: ƒ 2.50
Adults: ƒ 3.50

LELYSTAD

Museum Nieuwland
Oostvaardersdijk 01-13
8242 PA Lelystad
tel: 0320 - 260799

Opening hours:
Monday to Friday: 10 am to 5 pm.
Saturday, Sunday and public
holidays: 11:30 am to 5 pm.

Admission fees:
Children until 16: ƒ 4
Adults: ƒ 8.50
65+: ƒ 7.50
Annual season museum ticket
holders: free

DELTA-WORKS

Delta Expo Neeltje Jans
Oosterscheldedam / Postbus 19
4328 ZG Burgh-Haamstede
tel: 0111 - 652702

Opening hours:
Daily from 10 am to 5 pm.
November to March: Closed on
Mondays and Tuesdays.

Admission fees:
November to February:
Children until 3: free.
Children until 12: ƒ 7.50
Adults: ƒ 12.50
65+: ƒ 7.50
March to October:
Children until 3: free.
Children until 12: ƒ 11.50
Adults: ƒ 16.50
65+: ƒ 7.50

MIDDELBURG

Tourist Information
(ANWB/VVV) Middelburg:
Nieuwe Burg 40
4331 AH Middelburg
Organisation: 0118 - 659944
Information: 0118 - 659900

Zeeland Museum
(Zeeuws Museum)
Abdij 4
4331 BK Middelburg
tel: 0118 - 626655

Opening hours:
Monday to Friday: 11 am to 5 pm.
Sunday: noon to 5 pm.

Admission fees:
Children until 2: free
Children until 12: ƒ 2
Adults: ƒ 7
65+: ƒ 5.50
Annual season museum ticket
holders: free

'S HERTOGENBOSCH

Tourist Information (VVV)
Markt 77
5211 JX 's Hertogenbosch
tel: 0900 - 1122334
(ƒ 0.75 per minute)

Opening hours:
Monday to Friday:
9 am to 5:30 pm.
Saturday: 9 am to 4 pm.

page 121
St. John's Cathedral (St. Jan)
Torenstraat 16
5211 KK 's Hertogenbosch
tel: 0900 - 1122334

Opening hours (apart from masses):
From Easter to 3 November:
Daily: 8 am to 5 pm.
From 3 November to Easter:
Daily from 9:30 am to 4 pm.

There is no admission fee

MAASTRICHT

Tourist Information (VVV)
Kleine Staat 1
6211 ED Maastricht
tel: 043 - 3252121

page 124
St. Servaas Church
Keizer Karelplein 3
6211 TC Maastricht
tel: 043 - 3210490

Opening hours:
July and August:
Daily from 10 am to 6 pm.
August to June: 10 am to 5 pm.

Admission fees:
Children until 11: ƒ 1
Adults: ƒ 4
65+: ƒ 3

page 124
St. John's Church (St. Janskerk)
Vrijthof 24
6211 LE Maastricht
tel: 043 - 3216551

Opening hours:
From April to October:
Monday to Saturday: 10 am to 4 pm.

Admission fees:
Visiting the church is free
Mounting the tower: ƒ 2.50

page 125
Bonnefantenmuseum
Avenue Céramique 250
6221 KX Maastricht
tel: 043 - 3290190

Opening hours:
Tuesday to Sunday: 11 am to 5 pm.
Closed on: 25 December,
1 January and Carnival

Admission fees:
Children until 3: free
Children until 11: ƒ 7.50
Students: ƒ 7.50
Adults: ƒ 10
65+: ƒ 7.50
Annual season museum ticket
holders: free

PHOTOGRAPHY BY

Hans Slijpen, Amsterdam: page 6, 8, 9, 11, 18, 20, 41, 97, 128, 129, 129, 132, 150.

Johan van Rekom, Amsterdam: page 1, 2, 3, 7, 14, 17, 18, 21, 26, 27, 28, 32, 33, 34, 35, 36, 40, 45, 51, 52, 56, 58, 59, 60, 63, 64, 65, 70, 71, 72, 73, 74, 77, 79, 80, 81, 82, 84, 96, 98, 100, 105, 106, 107, 128, 148, 149.

Henk van der Leeden, Marken: page 9, 60, 78, 79, 80, 84, 86, 87, 94, 101.

Piet van der Meer, Amsterdam: page 4, 17, 22, 24, 25, 36.

Rijksvoorlichtingsdienst (Foto Thuring), Den Haag: page 3, 50.

Amsterdams Historisch Museum, Amsterdam: page 10, 14.

Nederlands Bureau voor Toerisme, Leidschendam: page 15, 21, 62, 78, 93.

Aerophoto Schiphol B.V., Schiphol: page 55, 72, 109, 116.

KLM Aerocarto, Schiphol: page 12, 114.

Nederlands Scheepvaartmuseum, Amsterdam: page 16.

Maarten Brinkgreve, Amsterdam: page 19.

Museum van Loon, Amsterdam: page 19.

Mauritshuis, Den Haag: page 22, 38, 49, 59, 130.

Museum Amstelkring, Amsterdam: page 22, 23.

Anne Frankstichting, Amsterdam: page 28, 29.

Portugees-Israelitische Gemeente, Amsterdam: page 30.

Bibliotheca Rosenthaliana, Amsterdam: page 30.

Coster Diamonds B.V., Amsterdam: page 31.

Gassan Diamonds, Amsterdam: page 31.

Rijksmuseum, Amsterdam: page 38, 40.

Rijksmuseum Vincent Van Gogh, Amsterdam: page 42, 43.

N.V. Nationale Luchthaven Schiphol: page 44.

Klompenmakerij Zaanse Schans, Zaandam: page 46, 47, 97.

Albert Heijn, Zaandam: page 47.

Molenmuseum Zaandijk: page 46.

Molen de Kat, Zaandam: page 47.

Anton van Daal, Westzaan: page 46.

Stichting Promotie Den Haag: page 48, 50, 51, 52.

Panorama Mesdag, Den Haag: page 52.

NBT Capital Press, Leidschendam: page 53.

Stichting Madurodam, Den Haag: page 54.

Fotostudio E. Boeijinga, Apeldoorn: page 55.

Eurocolor Creative, Sleewijk: page 57.

Aardewerkfabriek de Delftse Pauw, Delft: page 57.

Stedelijk Museum Het Prinsenhof, Delft: page 58.

Jurjen Drent, Haastrecht: page 59.

Paul Martens, Nieuwerkerk aan de IJssel: page 60.

Jan van der Ploeg, Rotterdam: page 61, 63.

VVV Rotterdam: page 61, 62.

Marco de Nood, Dordrecht: page 63.

Martin Droog, Gouda: page 64, 66.

VVV Gouda: page 64, 65.

Stichting Goudse Glazen, Gouda: page 66, 67.

Fotodienst Gemeente Utrecht: page 68, 69.

VVV Naarden: page 72.

Comenius Mausoleum Naarden: page 73.

Frans Halsmuseum, Haarlem: page 75.

VVV Alkmaar: page 76.

Wil Tjoa, Edam (via VVV Edam): page 81, 82, 83.

Hotel Spaander, Volendam: page 85.

Többen, Volendam: page 85.

Internationaal Bloembollen Centrum, Hillegom: page 88, 89.

Keukenhof, Lisse: page 90, 91.

VBA, Aalsmeer: page 92.

Kaasboerderij de Jacobshoeve, Katwoude: page 94, 95.

Maarten Udema, Amsterdam: page 96.

Ministerie Verkeer & Waterstaat, Den Haag: page 86, 98, 98, 111, 114, 117.

Pieter Cornelisz Cort, Alkmaar: page 99.

Boudewijn Ietswaart, Amsterdam: page 102, 103, 113.

Lemke (via NBT): page 106.

Rijksdienst IJsselmeerpolders, Lelystad: page 108.

Jan Blom, Lelystad: page 110.

Provincie Flevoland, Lelystad: page 111.

Jaap Wolterbeek, Middelburg: page 112, 115, 118, 119.

Provinciale VVV Zeeland, Middelburg: page 119.

VVV 's Hertogenbosch: page 120.

Ernst van Mecklenbergh, Rosmalen: page 121.

Anton van Horen, Heusden: page 122.

Philips N.V., Eindhoven: page 122.

Foto v.d. Ketelaar, Oirschot: page 123.

Fotogenique, Maastricht: page 124, 125, 126, 127.

Studio Koenders: page 129.

EDITORIAL

Written by:
Johan van Rekom

Design:
Anja Lanphen, Amsterdam

Lithography:
RVA, Amsterdam

Print:
Brouwer Groep, Utrecht.

Translation by:
Sander Bartling

1998 Uitgeverij P. Suurland
© Uitgeverij P. Suurland
Maasdrielhof 98
1106 NA Amsterdam / Holendrecht
tel: 020 - 6961051

CIP-Gegevens Koninklijke Bibliotheek:
Johan van Rekom.
Holland and Amsterdam. 150 pg.
ISBN:
90-803854-3-3

De praktische informatie is gebaseerd op de gegevens, zoals die in de zomer van 1998 door
de betreffende instanties verstrekt zijn.

Deze uitgave verschijnt in het Nederlands, Engels, Frans, Duits, Spaans,
Italiaans, Tsjechisch, Russisch, Chinees, Japans.